A Tankard of ale, an Anthology of Drinking Songs;

A TANKARD OF ALE

A TANKARD OF ALE

AN ANTHOLOGY OF DRINKING SONGS

COMPILED AND EDITED

BY

THEODORE MAYNARD

ERSKINE MACDONALD, LTD.

LONDON, W.C. 1

TO ALL GOOD FELLOWS WITH WHOM I HAVE DRUNK
AND TO ALL WHO HAVE DRUNK WITH ME

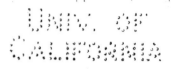

INTRODUCTION [1]

I

WITH the advent of the social reformer the very word
' beer ' seems to have taken on a sinister sound, and is
as much tabooed in polite society as the word ' trousers '
was once said to have been. This harmless and refresh-
ing drink has become credited with the most devilish
properties and characteristics, so that when it has to be
discussed (and Heaven only knows how much the thought
of it disturbs the minds of meddlesome philanthropists !)
it must be referred to under the alias of ' alcohol ' or
' the drinking habits of the lower classes.' Officialdom
has beer on the brain—which is quite the wrong place
for beer to be.

There is little wonder then that convivialty is a lost
art and that in consequence the making of drinking songs
has suffered a bad decline. ' Simon the Cellarer,' it is
true, may still be allowed even among Nonconformists,
but as it deals with ' Sack ' and ' Canary ' no real Puritan
objection can be raised. In fact these somewhat heady

---

[1] The publication of this anthology having been deferred till
the end of the War the first section of this Introduction has
already been included in a volume of my essays, " Carven from
the Laurel Tree," published February, 1919, by Mr. B. H.
Blackwell.

9

liquors are very probably considered to be teetotal drinks
—like Port. At any rate there is a pleasant and redeeming
smack of archaism about their names. *Beer*, however, is
quite another matter. One may only sing of *that* in a
music-hall—and not too often even there.

Very delightful verses are still occasionally written
about drinking, but generally these efforts have a purely
literary inspiration and cannot be honoured with the
name of drinking songs. Thus Charles Stuart Calverley
wrote, somewhere about the middle of last century, an
elaborate treatise upon ' that mild, luxurious, and artful
beverage, beer.' Yet in spite of the ode's noble apos-
trophe :

> " Oh Beer ! Oh Hodgson, Guinness, Allsopp, Bass !
> Names that should be on every infant's tongue ! "

we feel that Calverley's main interest lies in his poem
rather than in his tankard. The elegant undergraduate
speaks rather than the toper.

And Mr. Housman, carolling :

> " Malt does more than Milton can
> To reconcile God's ways to man,"

seems to find more satisfaction in a happy alliteration
than in his ale. He may be writing about malt—
but the maltworm's note is absent.

More recently the mild Mr. Masefield has led his
swaggering pirates on the stage, decked with striped
jerseys and cutlasses and (that nothing be lacking in their
artistic get-up) full of rum.

Introduction

" 'Oh some are fond of fiddles and a song well sung,
    And some are all for music that you lilt upon the tongue,
    But mouths were made for tankards and for sucking at
        the bung,'
            Says the old, bold mate of Henry Morgan."

The unfortunate thing about this cheerful poem is that
pirates do not talk like this—at least none of the pirates
that I know do so.

Then Robert Louis Stevenson once created a pirate—
not so gory and blasphemous as those who stalk about in
Mr. Masefield's pages, but a very nice pirate all the same.
Still, I don't think that :

    " Fifteen men on the dead man's chest—
        Yo-ho ! ho ! and a bottle of rum,"

was exactly the kind of observation that John Silver and
his companions would have been likely to make.

Songs of this type are all either offered with apologetic
humorousness or an equally . apologetic braggadocio.
None of them come within miles of catching the simple
seriousness of the genuine boozer. With hardly an excep-
tion, modern drinking songs appear to have been written
either out of pleasant affectation or in order to point a
moral. Beer was not made to be moralised about, but
to be drunk.

Those old drinking songs, in which the English language is so happily rich, are in a different class.
Among all their countless numbers there is no trace of
such a thing as self-consciousness. They were not written
to prove that beer ought to be consumed, but merely to

celebrate the fact of its consumption. Shamefacedness
or defence are entirely lacking in them. The only thing
to be uttered is a pæan of praise for a material blessing
joyfully accepted.

> " Back and side go bare, go bare !
> Both foot and hand go cold !
> But, belly, God send thee good ale enough
> Whether it be new or old."

So wrote Bishop Still in the sixteenth century. But
to-day we would draw long faces at such reprehensible
remarks and talk solemnly about less beer and more boots
—which is about as sensible as demanding less sun and
more sandwiches ! Perfect social reform casteth out
conviviality.

I wonder what our advocates of intemperate teetotalism
would say to this rollicking chorus :

> " I cannot go home, nor I will not go home—
> It's long of the oyle of Barley ;
> I'll tarry all night for my delight
> And go home in the morning early."

Such a note of vulgar human fellowship would be
certain to scorch Mr. Cadbury's ears, could they
hear it. Indeed, I often wonder whether it is not the
fellowship that he objects to even more than its companion drink. Did he but walk down Fleet Street
arm-in-arm with Mr. Gardiner and Dr. Clifford, the
three of them bawling out :

> " Tea ! Tea ! Glorious Tea ! "

Introduction

at the top of their voices, what man is there would not
join in ? Why cannot they sing :

> " Come pass the ginger-pop around
> And let us wet our noses ;
> It is the finest nectar found
> Since Noah or since Moses—
> With my iddly-ow : ti-rumpity-dow,
> Since Noah or since Moses ! "

at a P.S.A. with Mr. Arthur Henderson booming in with
a stentorian bass, and Mr. Philip Snowden with a
ringing tenor ? On the day that they do . . . ten
million converts will flock to their cause.

But alas ! the teetotallers have triumphed ! If they
have not altogether succeeded in putting down beer (in
their sense of the term), they have at least succeeded in
throwing a blight over our songs. If we have not become
sober, we have become sad—and that is something !
Mr. Chesterton has to ask plaintively who will write us
a drinking song, and, upon getting no replies, has to set
to work himself. But, though writing some glorious
verses in his attempt, he has on the whole failed through
his inability to forget the earnest face of the Puritan,
whose pale disgust is like a skeleton at his feast. He too
is the victim of his environment. How can he sing the
songs of Zion beside the waters of Babylon ? Beer, to
him, has ceased to be merely beer—but has become the
touchstone of economics, politics, and philosophy—so
that the whole of our modern contempt for the poor
can be set against the drinking of one honest half-pint.

A Tankard of Ale

" I knew no harm of Bonaparte and plenty of the Squire,
And for to fight the Frenchman I did not much desire ;
But I did bash their baggonets because they came
arrayed
To straighten out the crooked road an English drunkard
made,
Where you and I went down the lane with ale-mugs in
our hands,
The night we went to Glastonbury by way of Goodwin
sands."

Even here the facts of the French Revolution and the
tyranny of the countryside have to be dragged in, and
the whole history of England flung down as a challenging
gage.
One of the few genuine modern drinking songs was
made when Mr. Belloc wrote :

" If I should be what I never shall be,
    The Master or the Squire ;
If you gave me the hundred from here to the sea,
    Which is more than I desire,
Then all my crops should be barley and hops,
    And did my harvest fail,
I would sell every rood of my acres I would
    For a bellyful of good ale."

But even Mr. Belloc can rarely achieve anything so
single-minded as this. In an age of unbelief he has to
testify to eternal truth with a rousing bar-parlour chorus,
and lays his tankard about him as a truncheon in defence
of the Catholic Church :

Introduction

" So thank the Lord for the temporal sword,
   And for howling heretics too,
   And for all the good things that our Christendom
     brings,
   But especially barley brew ! "

It is perfectly true that wine is intimately, although obscurely, connected with the Faith, and Mr. Belloc is quite right when he shouts out at the top of his voice that barley brew is one of the good things that we owe to Christendom ; but this, though consoling to the soul and clarifying to the mind, certainly makes our drinking songs complicated. The boozer's thoughts ought to be on his pot—not on the Pope. But what with having Catholicism bellowed in at one ear and Puritanism snuffled in at the other, the poor man in the pub must get sorely distracted at times. Cannot he be left alone with his beer in peace ?

II

In this book I have tried (I trust successfully) to offer to my readers practically the whole cream of our convivial songs. But since a man must set a limit to his work, I tried to omit everything that was not English in its spirit and in its authorship. So strict a line being impossible, I have compromised to the extent of admitting poems by Scotsmen and Irishmen, while excluding their work when in dialect. It was, however, with real sorrow that I had to stop my ears to the rollicking chorus of Burns :

A Tankard of Ale

"We are na fu'; we are na fu';
But just a drappie in the ee.
The cock may craw; the day may daw—
But still we'll drink the barley bree."

I have made no attempt to preserve an exact chronological order, but have arranged the songs in what is the most satisfactory sequence that I could devise.

The notes are reduced to a minimum, for while many interesting ones might have been made, this book is rather intended for tapsters than for antiquaries—for those who would drink sack (were any to be had) rather than for those who propound learned theories as to what it really was.

In many instances a song has been reproduced before in several collections. In such cases I have contented myself with merely indicating *one* of the works where it may be found. Among the numerous books and broadsheets consulted in the compilation of my anthology I may mention the following: "The Percy Society's Edition of Songs and Carols"; "Chappell's Collections"; Evan's "Old Ballads"; "The Roxburghe Ballads"; D'Urfey's "Pills to Purge Melancholy"; J. W. Ebsworth's Collections; Ashton's "Wit, Humour, and Satire of the Seventeenth Century"; Ritson's "Ancient Songs"; Robert Bell's "Ancient Poems, Ballads, and Songs of the English Peasantry"; W. T. Marchant's "In Praise of Ale"; and Sir Alexander Croke's "Essay on Rhyming Latin Verse." A special mention must be made of "Songs of the Vine," an admirable anthology compiled by the late William G. Hutchison

Introduction

and published in 1904 by Mr. A. H. Bullen. The copy-
right is now held by Messrs. Sidgwick and Jackson, Ltd.,
who, with what can only be described as extravagant
generosity, put the book at my disposal.

To the modern authors herein represented and to their
publishers my hearty thanks are due for their permission
to include so much. The following have by their
courtesy enabled me to offer to my readers not only the
best of the older drinking songs but also the best drinking
songs of our own day : Mr. Hilaire Belloc and his publishers, Messrs. Duckworth and Co. and Messrs. Thos.
Nelson and Sons ; Mr. E. C. Bentley ; Mrs. Cecil
Chesterson, who allowed me to use a ballade of the late
Cecil Chesterton ; Mr. G. K. Chesterton and his publishers, Messrs. Methuen and Co., Ltd., and Messrs.
Burns and Oates ; Mr. Gerald Cumberland ; Mr. Geoffrey
Howard ; Mr. John Masefield, whose permission was
confirmed by Mr. Elkin Mathews, who also gave permission for the reprinting of John Davidson's " Ballade
of the Cheshire Cheese," from the " Book of the Rhymers'
Club " ; Mr. Alfred Noyes and his publishers, Messrs.
Wm. Blackwood and Sons ; Mr. John Lane for two
poems by John Davidson and two by C. W. Dalmon ; and
Mr. T. Michael Pope for a poem and for many valuable
suggestions.

I would like to have been able to include an extract
from " A Shropshire Lad," but Professor A. E. Housman refuses all anthologists ; and Mr. Austin Dobson
has declined to consent to " The Maltworm's Madrigal "
appearing here. I regret both these omissions ; still
more do I regret the reason (given me by the author) for

the second of these refusals, which is that Mr. Dobson is a water-drinker of many years standing!

There are some good American drinking songs, but a Prohibitionist nation does not deserve to be represented in the jolliest book in the world.

III

Songs of any sort are the best of indications of the national spirit, and consequently the safest guide to history. Especially is this true of English drinking songs wherein are to be found all the good-humour and pugnacity of our race.

" Our ports like our hearts shall be open and free ;
    We scorn for to fly or entrench :
Take your liquor, my bucks, take your liquor with glee;
    Down with that and then down with the French "

is the right note.

In many of our drinking songs, moreover, we are not content with merely calling for the destruction of the French, but for French wines, and even of any drinks which do not happen to be our favourite tipple. The traditional English exclusiveness only too often wrecks the broad catholic spirit of :

" Then let us be merry, wash sorrow away !
Wine, beer and ale shall be drunk to-day."

The beer-drinker instead will thirst for the blood of the wine-bibber and *vice versa :*

18

Introduction

" Let us sing our own treasures, old England's good cheer,
  The profits and pleasures of stout British beer ;
  Your wine-tippling, dram-sipping fellows retreat,
  But your beer-drinking Briton can never be beat."

All our taverns ring with the praises of beer. The eternal
anthem is :

" I likes a drop of good beer, I does ! "

so that it is left to Mr. Masefield, with whom it is more
(I suspect) a matter of professional interest than of
genuine conviction, to tell us (the old sea-dog !) that
rum's alone the tipple ; while Mr. Belloc, mellow with
memories of French vineyards, sings :

" Burgundy's Burgundy all the year round."

But although beer is our national beverage and should
accordingly be praised by patriotic Englishmen (not to
mention the noble fellows who according to Mr. Lloyd
George helped to pay for the war with every glass they
drank), it must not be forgotten that when, with the
introduction of hops into this country, the brewing of
beer, as distinct from ale, was made possible, a despondent
rhymer was moved to write :

" Carp, Heresy, Hops and Beer
  All came into England in one year."

After all that poets have told us of the merits of ale
(for who ever heard tell of a teetotal bard worth his salt ?)
—of its potency, its bravery, its honour, its laughter, its
kindliness, its simplicity, its power to confute cranks and

A Tankard of Ale

mean men, its profundity, its wisdom, its health, its
robustness, its hopefulness, its generosity, its sum-total
of all perfection, can any be found to rebuke us for our
love? Yes. Unfortunately there are men so degraded
and inhuman as not only to reject it themselves but to
attempt also to prevent others from proving its goodness.
The political mind, which can only find a complex
solution (which by the way never does solve) for what it
euphemistically terms the "drink problem," always
misses what is direct and effective. For when such a
mind in its blundering yet sophisticated way perceives
that harm is often brought to the poor of our slums by
their drinking bad beer, it fatuously proceeds in the holy
name of Social Reform to set wrong right by making
beer worse and by forbidding the poor to treat their
friends in a pub!

> Damn their eyes if ever they tries
> To rob a poor man of his beer—
> For I likes a drop of good beer.

THEODORE MAYNARD.

CONTENTS

A Tankard of Ale

Contents

23

A Tankard of Ale

Contents

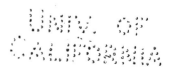

REASONS FOR DRINKING

By Henry Aldrich (1647–1710)

Si bene commemini causae sunt quinque bibendi—
Hospitis adventus, praesens sitis, atque futura,
Aut vini bonitas, aut quae libet altera causa.

If all be true that I do think,
There are five reasons we should drink :
Good wine—a friend—or being dry—
Or lest we should be by-and-by—
Or any other reason why.

BACK AND SIDE GO BARE, GO BARE![1]

By John Still
Bishop of Bath and Wells (1543 ?–1608)

Back and side go bare, go bare !
  Both foot and hand grow cold ;
But belly, God send thee good ale enough,
  Whether it be new or old.

---

[1] Still's version is a modernisation of a much older song, which may be found in the Percy Society's edition of Festive Songs. A Latin translation by Dr. Maginn is on pages 183-4.

27

A Tankard of Ale

I cannot eat but little meat,
    My stomach is not good;
But sure I think that I can drink
    With him that wears a hood.
Though I go bare, take ye no care,
    I nothing am a-cold.
I stuff my skin so full within
    Of jolly good ale and old.
      Back and side go bare, go bare!
      Both foot and hand grow cold;
    But belly, God send thee good ale enough,
      Whether it be new or old.

I have no roast but a nut-brown toast,
    And a crab laid in the fire;
A little bread shall do me stead,
    Much bread I do not desire.
No frost nor snow, nor wind I trow,
    Can hurt me if I wold;
I am so wrapped, and thoroughly lapped,
    Of jolly good ale and old.
      Back and side go bare, etc.

And Tib my wife, that as her life
    Loveth well good ale to seek,
Full oft drinks she, till ye may see
    The tears run down her cheek:
Then doth she trowl to me the bowl,
    Even as a maltworm should,
And saith, Sweetheart, I took my part
    Of this jolly good ale and old.
      Back and side go bare, etc.

28

A Catch, in Four Parts

Then let them drink till they nod and wink,
    Even as good fellows should do ;
They shall not miss to have the bliss
    Good ale doth bring men to :
And all poor souls that have scoured bowls,
    Or have them lustily trowled,
God save the lives of them and their wives,
    Whether they be young or old.
        Back and side go bare, etc.

A CATCH, IN FOUR PARTS[1]

By Thomas Shadwell (1640–1692)

Come, lay by your cares, and hang up your sorrow ;
Drink on, he's a sot that e'er thinks on to-morrow ;
Good store of good claret supplies everything,
And the man that is drunk is as great as a king.

Let none at misfortune or losses repine,
But take a full dose of the juice of the vine ;
Diseases and troubles are ne'er to be found,
But in the damned place where the glass goes not round.

[1] From " The Miser."

COME, LANDLORD, FILL A FLOWING BOWL [1]

COME, landlord, fill a flowing bowl, until it does run over ;
To-night we all will merry be, To-morrow we'll get sober.

He that drinks strong beer and goes to bed mellow,
Lives as he ought to live, and dies a hearty fellow.

Punch cures the gout, the cholic and the tisic,
And is to all men the very best of physic.

He that drinks small beer, and goes to bed sober,
Falls as the leaves do that die in October.

He that drinks strong beer and goes to bed mellow,
Lives as he ought to live, and dies a happy fellow.

He that courts a pretty girl, and courts her for her
  pleasure,
Is a fool to marry her without a store of treasure.

Now let us dance and sing, and drive away all sorrow
For perhaps we may not meet again to-morrow.

[1] From a Broadsheet in the British Museum. Circa, 1750.

A HEALTH TO ALL GOOD FELLOWES[1]

or

THE GOOD COMPANION'S ARITHMATICKE

Be merry, my hearts, and call for your quarts,
And let no liquor be lacking,
We have gold in store, we purpose to roare,
Untill we set care a-packing.
There, Hostesse, make haste, and let no time waste,
Let every man have his due,
To save shooes and trouble, bring in the pots double,
For he that made one made two.

I'll drink up my drink, and speak what I think,
Strong drink will make us speak truely,
We cannot be termed all drunkards confirmed,
So long as we are not unruly.
We'll drink and be civil, intending no evil.
If none be offended at me,
As I did before, so I'll add one more
And he that made two made three.

The greedy curmudgin sits all the day snudging
At home with brown bread and small beare,
To coffer up wealth, he starved himselfe,
Scarce eats a good meale in a year,

[1] From Roxburghe Ballads " to the tune of " To drive the old winter away." (Attributed to Martin Parker, circa 1560).

A Tankard of Ale

But I'll not do so, how ere the world go
  So long as I've money in store
I scorne for the faile, go fils up more Ale,
  For he that made three made four.

Why sit you thus sadly, because I call madly,
  I mean not to leave in the lurch,
My reckoning I'll pay ere I go away,
  Else hang me as high as a Church.
Perhaps you will say, this is not the way,
  They must pine that in this world will thrive;
No matter for that, we'll laugh and be fat,
  For he that made four made five.

To those my good friend my love so extends,
  I cannot truly express it ;
When with you I meet, your words are so sweet,
  I am unwilling to misse it.
I hate all base slaves that their money saves,
  And all those that use base tricks, ·
For with jovial blades, I'm merry as the Maids,
  For he that made five made six.

Then drink round about till sorrow be drowned,
  And let us sing hey downe a derry,
I cannot insure, to sit thus demure,
  For hither I came to be merry.
Then pluck up good heart before we depart,
  With my Hostesse we will make it even, ·
For I am set a madding, and still will be adding,
  For he that made six made seven.

A Health to All Good Fellowes

Sad melancholy will bring us folly,
    And this is death's principal magnet,
But this course I will take it never shall make,
    Me look otherwise than an agent.
And in more content my time shall be spent,
    And I'll pay every man his right,
Then, Hostesse, go fill, and stand not so still,
    For he that made seven made eight.

At home I confesse, with my wife honest Besse,
    I practise good husbandry well,
I follow my calling, to keep me from falling ;
    My neighbours about me that dwell.
Will praise me at large for maintaining my charge,
    But when I to drinking incline
I scorn for to shrinke, go fetch us more drinks,
    For he that made eight made nine.

Then while we are here, we'll drink Ale and Beer,
    And freely our money we'll spend
Let no man take care for paying his share,
    If need be I'll pay for my friend.
Then, Hostesse, make haste, and let no time waste,
    You're welcome all, kind Gentlemen,
Never fear to carouse, while there's beer in the house,
    For he that made nine made ten.

Then, Hostesse, be quicker, and bring us more liquor,
    And let no attendance be missing,
I cannot content me, to see the pot empty,
    A full cup is well worth the kissing.

c   33

A Tankard of Ale

Then, Hostesse, go fetch us some, for till you do come,
  We are of all joyes bereaven,
You know what I mean, make haste come again,
  For he that made ten made eleven.

With merry solaces, quite voyd of all malice,
  With honest good fellows that's here,
No cursing nor swearing, no staring nor tearing,
  Amongst us do serve to appeare.
When we have spent, all to labour we fall,
  For a living we'll dig or we'll delve,
Determined to be both bounteous and free,
  He that made eleven made twelve.

Now I think it is fit and most requisite,
  To drink a health to our wives,
The which being done, we'll pay and be gone,
  Strong drinke all our wits now deprives.
Then, Hostesse, let's know the summe that we owe,
  Twelve pence there is for certain,
Then t'other pot, and here's money for't,
  For he that made twelve made thirteen.

The Merry Fellows

THE MERRY FELLOWS [1]

Now, since we're met, let's merry, merry be,
  In spite of all our foes ;
And he that will not merry be,
  We'll pull him by the nose.
    Let him be merry, merry there,
      While we're all merry, merry here ;
      For who can know where he shall go
        To be merry another year ?

He that will not merry, merry be,
  With a generous bowl and a toast,
May he in Bridewell be shut up
  And fast bound to a post.
    Let him be merry, etc.

He that will not merry, merry be,
  And take his glass in course,
May he be obliged to drink small beer,
  Ne'er a penny in his purse.
    Let him be merry, etc.

He that will not merry, merry be,
  With a company of jolly boys,
May he be plagued with a scolding wife
  To confound him with her noise,
    Let him be merry, etc.

[1] From Bell's " Poems Ballads and Songs of the English Peasantry."

A Tankard of Ale

He that will not merry, merry be,
    With his sweetheart by his side,
Let him be laid in the cold churchyard
    With a headstone for his bride.
        Let him be merry, merry there,
            While we're all merry, merry here;
        For who can know where he shall go
            To be merry another year?

HERMIT HOAR, IN SOLEMN CELL

By Samuel Johnson (1709–1784)

" Hermit hoar, in solemn cell,
    Wearing out life's evening gray,
Smite thy bosom, sage, and tell,
    What is bliss, and which the way? "

Thus I spoke and speaking sighed,
    Scarce repressed the starting tear;
When the willing sage replied—
    " Come, my lad, and drink some beer ! "

WITH AN HONEST OLD FRIEND

By Henry Carey (d. 1743)

With an honest old friend and a merry old song,
And a flask of old port let me sit the night long,
And laugh at the malice of those who repine
That they must drink porter whilst I can drink wine.

36

Song of the Mug

I envy no mortal though ever so great,
Nor scorn I a wretch for his lowly estate ;
But what I abhor and esteem as a curse,
Is poorness of spirit, not poorness of purse.

Then dare to be generous, dauntless and gay,
Let us merrily pass life's remainder away ;
Upheld by our friends, we our foes may despise,
For the more we are envied, the higher we rise.

SONG OF THE MUG [1]

If Sorrow, the tyrant, invade the breast,
  Haul out the foul fiend by the lug, the lug !
Let no thought of the morrow disturb your rest,
  But banish despair in a mug, a mug !

Or if business, unluckily, goes not well,
  Let the fond fools their affections hug ;
To show our allegiance we'll go to " The Bell,"
  And banish despair in a mug, a mug !

Or if thy wife prove none of the best,
  Or admits no time but to think, to think,
Or the weight of the horns bow down thy crest,
  Divert the dull Demon with drink, with drink !

Or if thy mistress proves unworthy to thee,
  Ne'er pine, ne'er pine at the wanton pug ;

[1] From " Songs of the Vine."

37

A Tankard of Ale

But choose out a fairer and kinder than she,
  And banish despair in a mug, a mug!

From thee such pleasant joys, liquor, does flow,
  Which cures the distemper of heart and mind;
Our wits, O, then more riper do grow,
  By perfect experience the same we find.

Then he is an ass that seems to despair
  At any coy frown of the wanton pug;
Be merry and jolly, and drown all thy care
  For ever and aye in a mug, a mug!

As for the liquor, the juice of the grape
  Which often does into men's noddles creep,
And sometimes it makes them as wise as an ape,
  And sometimes it lays, like stocks, to sleep.

But whilst we are more sober and civil than they,
  Like brothers together in friendship hug,
And ever account it our duty to pay
  A worthy respect to the mug, the mug!

As for the spirit and juice of malt,
  It ripens the fancy of men enough,
And he is an ass that pretends to find fault
  With English because of their potent talk.

There's nothing more choice in all our land,
  To make a young gallant both brisk and smug,
And therefore no longer disputing we'll stand,
  But ever admire the mug, the mug!

38

MAKE ME A BOWL

By John Oldham (1653–83)

Make me a bowl, a mighty bowl,
Large as my capacious soul ;
Vast as my thirst is, let it have
Depth enough to be my grave ;
I mean the grave of all my care,
For I design to bury it there.
Let it of silver fashion'd be,
Worthy of wine, worthy of me !
Worthy to adorn the spheres
As that bright cup amongst the stars :
That cup which Heaven deign'd a place
Next the sun its greatest grace.
Kind cup ! that to the stars did go
To light poor drunkards here below ;
Let mine be so, and give me light ;
That I may drink and revel by't :
Yet draw no shapes of armour there,
No casque, nor shield, nor sword, nor spear.
Nor wars of Thebes, nor wars of Troy,
Nor any other martial toy :
For what do I vain armour prize,
Who mind not such rough exercise ?
But gentler sieges, softer wars,
Fights that cause no wounds or scars.
I'll have no battles on my plate,
Lets sight of them should brawls create ;

A Tankard of Ale

Lest that provoke to quarrels too,
Which wine itself enough can do.
Draw me no constellations there,
No Ram, nor Bull, nor Dog, nor Bear,
Nor any of that monstrous fry
Of animals, which stock the sky ;
For what are stars to my design ?
Stars which I, when drunk, outshine,
Outshone by every drop of wine :
I lack no pole-star on the brink,
To guide in the wide Sea of Drink ;
But would for ever there be tost,
And wish no haven, seek no coast.
Yet, gentle artist, if thou'lt try
Thy skill, then draw me (let me see),
Draw me first a spreading vine,
Make its arms the bowl entwine,
With kind embraces, such as I
Twist about my loving she.
Let its boughs o'erspread above
Scenes of drinking, scenes of love :
Draw next the patron of that tree,
Draw Bacchus, and soft Cupid by :
Draw them both in toping shapes ;
Their temples crown'd with clustered grapes ;
Make them lean against the cup,
As 'twere to keep the figures up ;
And when their reeling forms I view,
I'll think them drunk, and be so too.
   The gods shall my examples be,
   The gods thus drunk in effigy.

TOSSE THE POT

THOMAS RAVENSCROFT (1592–1635)

TOSSE the pot, tosse the pot, let us be merry,
And drink till our cheeks be red as a cherry.
We take no thought, we have no care,
For still we spend and never spare,
Till of all our money our purse is bare;
　　We ever tosse the pot.

　　　Chorus. Tosse the pot, tosse the pot, etc.

We 'drink, carous with hart most free,
A harty draught I drinke to thee ;
Then fill the pot again to me;
　　And ever tosse the pot.

　　　Chorus. Tosse the pot, etc.

And when our mony is all spent,
Then sell our goods and spend our rent,
Or drinke it up with one consent,
　　And ever tosse the pot.

　　　Chorus. Tosse the pot, etc.

When all is gone we have no more,
Then let us set it on the score,
Or chalk it up behinde the dore,
　　And ever tosse the pot.

　　　Chorus. Tosse the pot, etc.

41

A Tankard of Ale

And when our credit is all lost,
Then may we goe and kisse the post,
And eat browne bread in steed of rost,
    And ever tosse the pot.

    Chorus. Tosse the pot, etc.

Let us conclude as we began,
And tosse the pot from man to man,
And drinke as much now as we can,
    And ever tosse the pot.

Chorus. Tosse the pot, tosse the pot, let us be merry,
    And drinke till our cheeks be as red as a cherry.

ALL YOU THAT ARE GOOD FELLOWS [1]

ALL you that are good fellows,
    Come hearken to my song;
I know you do not hate good cheer,
    Nor liquor that is strong.
I hope there is none here,
    But soon will take my part,
Seeing my master and my dame
    Say welcome with their heart.

This is a time of joyfulness,
    And merry time of year,
When as the rich with plenty stored,
    Do make the poor good cheer.

[1] 1642. Chappell's Collection.

All You that are Good Fellows

Plum-porridge, roast beef, and minced pies
  Stand smoking as the board
With other brave varieties
  Our master doth afford.

Our mistress and her cleanly maids
  Have neatly played the cook,
Methinks those dishes eagerly
  At my sharp stomach look,
As though they were afraid
  To see me draw my blade ;
But I revenged on them will be,
  Until my stomach's stayed.

Come fill us of the strongest,
  Small drink is out of date,
Methinks I shall fare like a prince,
  And sit in gallant state :
This is no miser's feast,
  Although that things be dear ;
God grant the founder of this feast
  Each Christmas keep good cheer.

This day for Christ we celebrate,
  Who was born at this time ;
For which all Christians should rejoice,
  And I do sing in rhyme.
When you have given thanks
  Unto your dainties fall,
Heaven bless my master and my dame ;
  Lord bless me and you all.

A Tankard of Ale

'GOOD ALE FOR MY MONEY [1]

BY LAWRENCE PRICE (fl. 1625–1680?)

THE Good Fellows resolution of strong ale,
That cures his nose from looking pale.

Be merry, my Friends, and list a while
  Unto a merry jest ;
It may from you produce a smile,
  When you heare it expressed,—
Of a young man lately married,
  Which was a boone good fellow,
This song in his head he alwaies carried
  When drink had made him mellow :

  I cannot go home, nor I will not go home,
    It's long of the oyle of Barley ;
  I'll tarry all night for my delight,
    And go home in the morning early.

No Tapster stout, or Vintner fine,
  Quoth he, shall ever get
One groat out of this purse of mine,
  To pay his master's debt :
Why should I deal with starking Rookes,
  That seeke poor gulls to cozen,
To give twelve pence for a quart of wine ?
  Of ale 'twill buy a dozen.
    I cannot go home, etc.

[1] From the Roxburghe Ballads. To the tune of "The
Countrey Lasse."

44

Good Ale for my Money

The old renowned Ipocrist
  And Rapsie doth excell ;
But never any wine could yet
  My honour please to swell.
The Rhenish wine or muscadine,
  Sweet malmsie is too fulsome ;
No, give me a cup of Barlie broth,
  For that is very wholesome.
      I cannot go home, etc.

Hot waters are to me as death,
  And soone the head o?erturneth,
And nectar hath so strong a breath ;
  Canary when it burneth,
It cures no paine, but breaks the braine,
  And raps out oaths and curses,
And makes men; part with heavy heart—
  But light it makes their purses.
      I cannot go home, etc.

Some say Matheglin beares the name
  With Perry and sweet Sider ;
'Twill bring the body out of frame,
  And reach the belly wider ;
Which to prevent, I am content,
  With ale that's good and nappy,
And when thereof I have enough
  I think myself most happy.
      I cannot go home, etc.

A Tankard of Ale

All sorts of men, when they do meet,
　Both trade and occupation,
With curtesie each other greet,
　And kinde humiliation ;
A good coale fire is their desire,
　Whereby to sit and parly ;
They'll drink their ale, and tell a tale,
　And go home in the morning early.

　　I cannot go home, nor I will not go home,
　　　It's long of the oyle of Barley ;
　　I'll tarry all night for my delight,
　　　And go home in the morning early.

I AM THE JOLLY PRINCE OF DRINKERS [1]

　I AM the jolly prince of drinkers,
　　Ranting, roaring, fuddling boys !
Who take a delight in tossing full tankards,
　　Filling the ale-house with my noise.
Ten gallons at a draught
　　Did I pour down my throat.
But hang such silly sips as these :
　　I laid me all along
　　With my mouth unto the bung,
And I drank off a hogshead at my ease.

[1] From Horsfield's Vocal Music, 1775. In the Ministrelsy
of England, published by Bayley and Ferguson, the fine music
is easily accessible.

I am the Jolly Prince of Drinkers

I've heard that a fop who'd toss a full tankard
  Crowned himself the prince of sots ;
But hang such silly idle drunkards,
 Snatch their flagons, break their pots ;
My friend and I did join
For a cellar full of wine,
  And locked the vintner out of door.
One morning at the tap,
There we drank it every drop,
  And eagerly ranged about for more.

My friend to me did make a motion,
  " Must we part, and with dry lips ? "
Oh, then we went unto the ocean,
  Where we did meet a fleet of ships.
Their lading it was wine,
And that most superfine ;
  Their burden was ten hundred ton.
We drank it all at sea,
Long before we came to quay,
  And the merchants did swear they were undone.

And then we went to the Canaries,
  Hoping to find a better touch ;
And there we did meet with Portuguese,
  Likewise the Spaniards and the Dutch.
'Twas near the river Rhine.
We drank up all the wine,

A Tankard of Ale

We thought to drink the ocean dry.
Bacchus swore he'd never found
In the universe all round
Two souls, such thirsty souls, as my friend and I.

THE WORLD DROWNED IN A GLASS [1]

WHAT need we take care for Platonical rules,
Or the precepts of Aristotle ;
Those that think to find learning in books are but fools,
True philosophy lies in the bottle :
And the mind that's confined to the modes of the schools
Ne'er arrives to the height of a pottle :
Let the sages, of our ages, keep a-talking of our walking,
Demurely, whilst we that are wiser
Do abhor all that's moral in Cato and Plato,
And Seneca talks like a sizer :
Then let full bowls, full bottles and bowls be hurled,
That our jollity may be completer :
For man, tho' he be but a very little world,
Must be drowned as well as the greater.

We will drink till our cheeks are as starred as the skies,
Let the pale-coloured student flout us ;
Till our noses, like comets, set fire on our eyes,
And we bear the horizon about us.
And if ale makes no fall, then our heels shall divine
What the stars are a-doing without us :

[1] From "Pills to Purge Melancholy."

48

Prithee Fill Me my Glass

Let Lilly go tell ye 'of thunders and wonders,
  And astrologers all divine ;
Let Booker be a looker in our natures and features,
  He'll find nothing but claret in mine !
Then let full bowls, full bottles and bowls be hurled,
  That our jollity may be completer :
For man, tho' he be but a very little world,
  Must be drowned as well as the greater.

PRITHEE FILL ME MY GLASS [1]

By William Congreve (1670–1729)

Prithee fill me my glass,
Till it laugh in my face,
With ale that is potent and mellow ;
  He that whines for a lass,
  Is an ignorant ass,
For a bumper has not its fellow. .

We'll drink, and we'll never ha' done, boys,
Put the glass then around with the sun, boys.
Let Apollo's example invite us ;
  For he's drunk every night,
  And that makes him so bright,
That he's able next morning to light us.

To drink is a Christian diversion
Unknown to the Turk or the Persian :
  Let Mahometan fools,
  Live by heathenish rules,

[1] From " The Way of the World."

D   49

A Tankard of Ale

And be damn'd over teacups and coffee ;
But let British lads sing,
Crown a health to the King.
And a fig for our Sultan and Sophy !

SONG FROM ".THE DUENNA"

By Richard Brinsley Sheridan (1751–1816)

Oh, the days when I was young.
  When I laugh'd in fortune's spite ;
Talk'd of love the whole day long,
  And with nectar crown'd the night !
. Then it was, old Father Care,
  Little reck'd I of thy frown ;
Half thy malice youth could bear,
  And the rest a bumper drown.

Truth, they say, lies in a well,
  Why, I vow I ne'er could see ;
Let the water-drinkers tell,
  There it always lay for me.
For when sparkling wine went round,
  Never saw I falsehood's mask ;
But still honest truth I found
  In the bottom of each flask.

THE TOPER'S RANT

By John Clare (1793–1864)

Come, come, my old crones and gay fellows
That love to drink ale in a horn,
We'll sing racy songs now we're mellow
Which topers sung ere we were born.
For our bottle kind fate shall be thankéd,
And line but our pockets with brass,
We'll sooner suck ale through a blanket
Than thimbles of wine from a glass.

Away with your proud thimble glasses
Of wine foreign nations supply,
We topers ne'er drink to the lasses
Over draughts scarce enough for a fly.
Club us with the hedger and ditcher
Or beggar that makes his own horn,
To join us o'er bottle or pitcher
Foaming o'er with the essence of corn.

We care not with whom we get tipsy
Or where with brown stout we regale,
We'll weather the storm with a gipsy
If he be a lover of ale.
We'll weather the toughest storm weary
Although we get wet to the skin,
If outside our cottage looks dreary
We're warm and right happy within.

A Tankard of Ale

We'll sit till the bushes are dropping
Like the spout of a watering-pan,
For till the dram's drank there's no stopping,
We'll keep up the ring to a man.
We'll sit till Dame Nature is feeling
The breath of our stingo so warm,
And bushes and trees begin reeling
In our eyes like to ships in a storm.

We'll sit for three hours before seven,
When larks wake the morning to dance,
Till night's sooty brood of eleven,
With witches ride over to France.
We'll sit it in spite of the weather
Till we tumble our length on the plain,
When the morning shall find us together,
To play the game over again.

BOOZE IS THERE [1]

WHERE the wintry winds are blowing,
    Booze is there !
Where the summer plants are growing,
    Booze is there !
In the desert or the ocean,
In the Cars of Locomotion,
Even in Sir Wilfrid's lotion,
    Booze is there !

[1] This song was published about 1890 by R. Maynard, 346 Hackney Road, E.   The " Sir Wilfrid " referred to is the late Sir Wilfrid Lawson, M.P.

Booze is There

In the opera, at the drama,
  Booze is there !
Sacred concerts, panorama,
  Booze is there !
On the hill and in the valley,
Open street or crowded alley,
Even in the spotless ballet,
  Booze is there !

In the parlour or the attic,
  Booze is there !
Royal drinks or democratic,
  Booze is there !
Where the School Board airs its teaching,
Even when the parson's preaching,
Or his flocks to pray beseeching,
  Booze is there !

When little stranger comes to town.
  Booze is there !
Mrs. Jones meets Mrs. Brown,
  And Booze is there !
The baby's praised right down to the ground,
Pronounced by all quite safe and sound,
Then once again the glass goes round,
  And Booze is there !

In climate cold or climate hot,
  Booze is there !
Even in granny's old teapot,
  Booze is there !

A Tankard of Ale

But travel fast or travel slow,
No matter a hang wherever you go,
To Chelsea or to Pimlico,
    Booze is there !

When you wed the girl of your heart,
    Booze is there !
The day you vow you ne'er will part,
    Booze is there !
In the palace, in the stable,
Since the days of Cain and Abel,
In every house, on every table, ·
    Booze is there !

THREE MEN OF GOTHAM [1]

By Thomas Love Peacock (1785–1866)

Seamen three ! what men be ye ?
    Gotham's three wise men we be.
Whither in your bowl so free ?
    To rake the moon from out the sea.
The bowl goes trim, the moon doth shine.
And our ballast is old wine ;
And your ballast is old wine.

Who art thou, so fast adrift ?
    I am he they call Old Care.
Here on board we will thee lift.
    No : I may not enter there.

[1] From "Nightmare Abbey."

Glee from "Headlong Hall"

Wherefore so ? 'Tis Jove's decree,
In a bowl Care may not be ;
In a bowl Care may not be.

Fear ye not the waves that roll ?
  No : in charmed bowl we swim.
What the charm that floats the bowl ?
  Water may not pass the brim.
The bowl goes trim, the moon doth shine.
And our ballast is old wine ;
And your ballast is old wine.

GLEE FROM "HEADLONG HALL"

BY THOMAS LOVE PEACOCK

A HEELTAP ! a heeltap ! I never could bear it !
So fill me a bumper, a bumper of claret !
Let the bottle pass freely, don't shirk it nor spare it,
For a heeltap ! a heeltap ! I never could bear it !

No skylight ! no twilight ! while Bacchus rules o'er us :
No thinking ! no shrinking ! all drinking in chorus :
Let us moisten our clay, since 'tis thirsty and porous :
No shrinking ! no shrinking ! all drinking in chorus !

55

A Tankard of Ale

SONG FROM "HEADLONG HALL"

BY THOMAS LOVE PEACOCK

In his last binn Sir Peter lies,
  Who knew not what it was to frown :
Death took him mellow, by surprise,
  And in his cellar stopped him down.
Through all the land we could not boast
  A knight more gay, more prompt than he,
To rise and fill a bumper toast,
  And pass it round with THREE TIMES THREE.

None better knew the feast to sway,
  Or keep mirth's boat in better trim ;
For Nature had but little clay
  Like that of which she moulded him.
The meanest guest that graced his board
  Was there the freest of the free,
His bumper toast when Peter poured,
  And passed it round with THREE TIMES THREE.

He kept at true good humour's mark
  The social flow of pleasure's tide :
He never made a brow look dark,
  Nor caused a tear, but when he died.
No sorrow round his tomb should dwell :
  More pleased his gay old ghost would be
For funeral song and passing bell,
  To hear no sound but THREE TIMES THREE.

56

Song

WE'LL DINE AND DRINK

(From Crochet Castle)

By Thomas Love Peacock

If I drink water while this doth last,
  May I never again drink wine :
For how can a man, in his life of a span,
  Do anything better than dine ?
We'll dine and drink, and say if we think
  That anything better can be ;
And when we have dined, wish all mankind
  May dine as well as we.

And though a good wish will fill no dish,
  And brim no cup with sack,
Yet thoughts will spring, as the glasses ring,
  To illumine our studious track.
On the brilliant dreams of our hopeful schemes
  The light of the flask shall shine ;
And we'll sit all day, but we'll find a way
  To drench the world with wine.

SONG

By Gerald Cumberland

A fool am I, for money slips
  Between my fingers ere the gold
Has time to traffic with my dreams,
  And litter actions manifold.

57

A Tankard of Ale

My silver cup has wide smooth lips,
    And loves to have a deep carouse ;
He winks the firelight in my eyes,
    And pours contempt on empty vows.

O ! warm to body, cool to throat,
    And fragrant to the lips is gay
And jolly Beaune, that sings a tune
    To stories of old Rabelais.

A fool am I, for wine is waste,
    And what the wise say I know well ;
That he who spends his days in song
    Will pass eternity in hell.

Whene'er I hold within my palms
    A kingdom or a world of bliss,
The golden darlings melt between
    My cup-shaped hands' interstices.

Full many a sovereign have I thrown
    Into the vats of Southern France,
And all my golden guineas fall
    Into the laps of Song and Dance.

And lean, long faces look at me,
    And prophesy an evil doom ;
But when my day of reckoning comes,
    I'll lie safe-housed within my tomb,

Cast Away Care

Knowing full well the sprite of me,
  Nourished by all my body's boon,
Is great and generous company
  For pale ghosts shiv'ring 'neath the moon.

CAST AWAY CARE [1]

By Thomas Dekker (1570?–1641?)

Cast away care; he that loves sorrow
Lengthens not a day, nor can buy to-morrow;
Money is trash; and he that will spend it,
Let him drink merrily, Fortune will send it.
  Merrily, merrily, merrily, oh, ho!
  Play it off stiffly, we may not part so.

Wine is a charm, it heats the blood too,
Cowards it will harm, if the wine be good too;
Quickens the wit, and makes the back able;
Scorn to submit to the watch or constable.
  Merrily, merrily, etc.

Pots fly about, give us more liquor,
Brothers of a rout, our brains will flow quicker;
Empty the cask; score it up we care not,
Fill up the pots again, and drink on and spare not.
  Merrily, merrily, etc.

[1] From "The Sun's Darling," by Ford and Dekker, 1623

A Tankard of Ale

DRINK TO-DAY [1]

BY JOHN FLETCHER (1579–1625)

DRINK to-day and drown all sorrow,
You shall perhaps not do it to-morrow :
Best, while you have it, use your breath ;
There'll be no drinking after death.

Wine works the heart up, wakes the wit,
There is no cure 'gainst age but it :
It helps the headache, cough and tisic,
And is for all diseases physic.

Then let us smile, boys, for our health ;
Who drinks well, loves the commonwealth ;
And he that will to bed go sober,
Falls with the leaf still in October.

DRINKING COMMENDED

BY SIR JOHN SUCKLING (1609–1642)

COME, let the State stay,
And drink away,
There is no business above it :
It warms the cold brain,
Makes us speak in high strain,
He's a fool that does not approve it.

[1] From the " Bloody Brothers, or Rollo, Duke of Normandy."

The Jovial Drinker

The Macedon youth,
Left behind him this truth,
That nothing is done with much thinking;
He drank and he fought,
Till he had what he sought :
The world was his own by good drinking.

THE JOVIAL DRINKER [1]

A PLAGUE on those fools who exclaim against wine,
And fly the dear sweets that the bottle doth bring;
It heightens the fancy, the wit does refine,
And he that was first drunk was made the first king.

By the help of good claret old age becomes youth,
And sick men still find this the only physician;
Drink largely, you'll know by experience the truth,
That he that drinks most is the best politician.

To victory this leads on the brave cavalier,
And makes all the terrors of war but delight;
This flushes his courage, and beats off base fear,
'Twas that that taught Cæsar and Pompey to fight.

This supports all our friends, and knocks down all our foes,
This makes all men loyal from courtier to clown;
Like Dutchman from brandy, from this our strength
    grows;
So 'tis wine, noble wine, that's a friend to the crown.

[1] From " Pills to Purge Melancholy."

A Tankard of Ale

THE TIPPLING PHILOSOPHERS [1]

Wise Thales, the father of all,
   The Greek philosophical crew,
Ere he gazed at the heavens would call
   For a chirruping bottle or two,
That, when he had brighten'd his eyes,
   He the planets might better behold,
And make the fools think he was wise,
   By the whimsical tales that he told.

Diogenes, surly and proud,
   Who snarl'd at the Macedon youth,
Delighted in wine that was good,
   Because in good wine there is truth ;
Till growing as poor as a Job,
   Unable to purchase a flask,
He chose for his mansion a tub,
   And liv'd by the scent of the cask.

Heraclitus would never deny
   A bumper to comfort his heart ;
And when he was maudlin would cry,
   Because he had emptied his quart :
Though some are so foolish to think
   He wept at man's folly and vice,
'Twas only his custom to drink
   Till the liquor flow'd out of his eyes.

[1] From " Wine and Wisdom, or The Tippling Philosophers,"
published 1710.

The Tippling Philosophers

Democritus always was glad
  To tipple and cherish his soul;
And would laugh like a man that was mad,
  When over a full flowing bowl:
As long as his cellar was stor'd,
  The liquor he'd merrily quaff;
And when he was drunk as a lord
  At those that were sober he'd laugh.

Wise Solon, who carefully gave
  Good laws unto Athens of old,
And thought the rich Crœsus a slave,
  Though a king, to his coffers of gold;
He delighted in plentiful bowls,
  But, drinking, much talk would decline,
Because 'twas the custom of fools
  To prattle much over their wine.

Old Socrates ne'er was content,
  Till a bottle had heighten'd his joys,
Who in's cups to the oracle went,
  Or he ne'er had been counted so wise
Late hours he certainly lov'd,
  Made wine the delight of his life,
Or Xantippe would never have proved
  Such a damnable scold of a wife.

Grave Seneca, fam'd for his parts,
  Who tutored the bully of Rome,
Grew wise o'er his cups and his quarts,
  Which he drank like a miser at home:

A Tankard of Ale

And to show he lov'd wine that was good
  To the last we may truly aver it,
That he tinctur'd the bath with his blood,
  So he fancied he died in his claret.

Pythag'ras did silence enjoin
  On his pupils, who wisdom would seek,
Because that he tippled good wine
  Till himself was unable to speak :
And when he was whimsical grown
  With sipping his plentiful bowls,
By the strength of the juice in his crown
  He conceiv'd transmigration of souls.

Copernicus, like to the rest,
  Believ'd there was wisdom in wine,
And fancied a cup of the best
  Made reason the brighter to shine ;
With wine he replenish'd his veins,
  And made his philosophy reel ;
Then fancied the world like his brains,
  Ran round like a chariot wheel.

Theophrastus, that eloquent sage,
  By Athens so greatly ador'd,
With a bottle would boldly engage,
  When mellow was brisk as a bird ;
Would chat, tell a story, and jest
  Most pleasantly over a glass,
And thought a dumb guest at a feast·
  But a dull philosophical ass.

64

The Tippling Philosophers

Anaxarchus, more patient than Job,
  By pestles was pounded to death,
Yet scorn'd that a groan or a sob
  Should waste the remains of his breath;
But sure he was free with the glass,
  And drank to a pitch of disdain,
Or the strength of his wisdom, alas!
  I fear would have flinch'd at the pain.

Aristotle, the master of arts,
  Had been but a dunce without wine,
And what we ascribe to his parts,
  Is due to the juice of the vine :
His belly, most writers agree,
  Was as large as a watering-trough;
He therefore jump'd into the sea,
  Because he'd have liquor enough.

When Pyrrho had taken a glass,
  He saw that no object appear'd
Exactly the same as it was
  Before he had liquor'd his beard;
For things running round in his drink,
  Which sober he motionless found,
Occasion'd the sceptic to think
  There was nothing of truth to be found.

Old Plato was reckon'd divine,
  He wisely to virtue was prone;
But had it not been for good wine,
  His merits we never had known.

E
65

A Tankard of Ale

By wine we are generous made,
It furnishes fancy with wings ;
Without it we ne'er should have had
·Philosophers, poets, or kings. ·

THE THREE PIGEONS

By Oliver Goldsmith (1728–1774)

Let schoolmasters puzzle their brain
With grammar and nonsense and learning,
Good liquor, I stoutly maintain,
Gives *genus* a better discerning. ·
Let them brag of their heathenish gods,
Their Lethes, their Styxes and Stygians,
Their *qui's* and their *quae's* and their *quods*.
They're all put a parcel of pigeons !
Toroddle, toroddle, toroll !

When Methodist preachers come down,
A-preaching that drinking is sinful,
I'll wager the rascals a crown
They always preach best with a skinful.
But when you come down with your pence
For a slice of their scurvy religion,
I'll leave it to all men of sense,·
But you, my good friend, are the pigeon.
Toroddle, toroddle, toroll !

66

Fill the Goblet Again

Then, come, put the jorum about,
  And let us be merry and clever,
Our hearts and our liquors are stout,
  Here's the Three Jolly Pigeons for ever !
Let some cry up woodcock or hare,
  Your bustards, your ducks, and your widgeons,
But of all the gay birds in the air,
    Here's a health to the Three Jolly Pigeons !
    Toroddle toroddle, toroll !

FILL THE GOBLET AGAIN

By Lord Byron (1788–1824)

Fill the goblet again ! for I never before
Felt the glow that now gladdens my heart to its core ;
Let us drink !—who would not ?—since through life's
  varied round
In the goblet alone no deception is found.

I have tried in its turn all that life can supply ;
I have basked in the beam of a dark rolling eye ;
I have loved !—who has not ?—but what heart can
  declare,
That pleasure existed whilst passion was there ?

In the bright days of youth, when the heart's in its
    spring,
And dreams that affection can never take wing,

67

A Tankard of Ale

I had friends !—who has not ?—but what tongue will
    avow,
That friends, rosy wine, are so faithful as thou ?

The heart of a mistress some boy may estrange ;
Friendship shifts with the sunbeam—thou never canst
    change ;
Thou grow'st old !—who does not ?—but on earth what
    appears,
Whose virtues, like thine, still increase with its years ?

Yet if blest to the utmost that love can bestow,
Should a rival bow down to our idol below,
We are jealous—who's not ?—thou hast no such alloy ;
For the more that enjoy thee, the more they enjoy.

Then the season of youth and its vanities past,
For refuge we fly to the goblet at last ;
There we find—do we not ?—in the flow of the soul,
That truth, as of yore, is confined to the bowl.

When the box of Pandora was opened on earth,
And Misery's triumph commenced over Mirth,
Hope was left—was she not ?—but the goblet we kiss,
And care not for Hope who are certain of bliss.

Long Life to the grape ! for when summer is flown,
The age of our nectar shall gladden our own ;
We must die—who shall not ?—may our sins be forgiven,
And Hebe shall never be idle in heaven !

Goldthred's Song

GOLDTHRED'S SONG [1]

BY SIR WALTER SCOTT (1771–1832)

OF all the birds on bush or tree,
  Commend me to the owl;
Since he may best ensample be
  To those the cup that trowl.
For when the sun hath left the west
He chooses the tree that he loves best,
And he whoops out his song, and he laughs at his jest.
  Though hours be late and weather foul,
  We'll drink to the health of the bonny owl.

The lark is but a bumpkin fowl,
  He sleeps in his nest till morn;
But my blessing upon the jolly owl,
  That all night blows his horn.
Then up wi' your cup till you stagger in speech,
And match me this catch till you swagger and screech
And drink till you wink, my merry men each.
  Though hours be late and weather foul,
  We'll drink to the health of the bonny owl.

[1] From " Kenilworth." A musical setting of this song is
published by Messrs. Boosey & Co.

LINES ON THE MERMAID TAVERN

By John Keats (1795–1821)

Souls of poets dead and gone,
What Elysium have ye known,
Happy field or mossy cavern,
Choicer than the Mermaid Tavern ?
Have ye tippled drink more fine
Than mine host's Canary wine ?
Or are fruits of Paradise
Sweeter than those dainty pies
Of venison ? · O generous food !
Drest as though bold Robin Hood
Would, ·with his maid Marian,
Sup and bowse from horn and can.

I have heard that on a day
Mine host's signboard fled away,
Nobody knew whither, till
An astrologer's old quill
To a sheepskin gave the story,
Said he saw you in your glory,
Underneath a new-old sign
Sipping beverage divine,
And pledging with contented smack
The Mermaid in the Zodiac.
Souls of poets dead and gone,
What Elysium have ye known,
Happy field or mossy cavern,
Choicer than the Mermaid Tavern ?

THE MERMAID INN [1]

Dekker's Song

By Alfred Noyes

THE Cardinal's Hat is a very good inn,
  And so is the *Puritan's Head ;*
But I know a sign of a wine, a wine
  That is better when all is said.
It is whiter than Venus, redder than Mars,
  It was old when the world begun ;
For all good inns are moons or stars,
  But the Mermaid is their Sun.

Chorus. They are all alight like moons in the night,
  But the Mermaid is their Sun.

Therefore when priest or parson cries
  That inns like flowers increase,
I say that mine inn is a church likewise,
  And I say to them " Be at peace ! "
An host may gather in dark St. Paul's
  To salve their souls from sin ;
But the light may be where " two or three "
  Drink wine in the *Mermaid Inn.*

Chorus. The Light may be where " two or three "
  Drink wine in the *Mermaid Inn.*

[1] From " Tales of the Mermaid Tavern."

ANACREONTIQUES, No. 2[1]

BY ABRAHAM COWLEY (1618–1667)

THE thirsty earth soaks up the rain,—
And drinks, and gapes for drink again.
The plants suck in the earth, and are
With constant drinking fresh and fair.
The sea itself (which one would think
Should have but little need to drink),
Drinks twice ten thousand rivers up,
So fill'd that they o'èrflow the cup.
The busy sun (and one would guess
By 's drunken fiery face no less),
Drinks up the sea, and, when he's done,
The moon and stars drink up the sun.
They drink and dance by their own light,
They drink and revel all the night.
Nothing in nature's sober found,
But an eternal health goes round.
Fill up the bowl, then, fill it high,
Fill all the glasses there; for why
Should every creature drink but I,
Why, man of mortals, tell me why?

[1] Tune in "Collection of Drinking Songs" at the British
Museum.

72

THE JOLLY BACCHANAL [1]

COME, all ye jolly Bacchanals,
  That love to tope good wine,
Let's offer up a hogshead
  Unto our Master's shrine,
Then let us drink and never shrink,
  For I'll tell you the reason why:
'Tis a great sin to leave a house
  'Till we've drained the cellar dry.

In times of old I was a fool,
  I drank the water clear,
But Bacchus took me from that rule;
  He thought 'twas too severe.
He fill'd a goblet to the brim,
  And he bade me take a sup,
And had it been a gallon pot,
  By Jove I'd tossed it up.

And ever since that happy time,
  Good wine has been my cheer.
Now nothing puts me in a swoon,
  But water or small beer;
Then let us tope about, my boys,
  And never flinch nor fly,
But fill our skins brimful of wine,
  And drain the bottles dry.

[1] From untitled collection in the British Museum. No name of writer or composer given.

A Tankard of Ale

COME, THOU MONARCH OF THE VINE [1]

By WILLIAM SHAKESPEARE (1564–1616)

Come, thou monarch of the vine,
Plumpy Bacchus with pink eyne!
In thy vats our cares be drown'd,
With thy grapes our hairs be crown'd :
  Cup us, till the world go round,
  Cup us, till the world go round !

BACCHUS

By HUGH CROMPTON [2]

Come, jolly god Bacchus, and open thy store,
  Let the big-belly'd grapes of their burden be eased,
Let thy liberality freely flow o'er,
  For 'tis by thy bounty that we are appeased :
    It is sack that we lack,
    It is sack that we crave ;
It is sack that we fight for, and sack we will have !

Let pining Heraclitus drink of his tear,
  And snivelling Tymon lie sick in his cell ;
And let the coarse bumpkin preach law in his beer ;
  But 'tis wine makes our fame and our glory to swell :
    It is wine makes divine,
    All our wits, and renowns,
The peasant with sceptres, the shepherd with crowns.

[1] From "Antony and Cleopatra."
[2] From "Pierides, or the Muses' Mount," 1658.

74

Bacchus

He that spends his money for honour, and climbs
 In the trees of triumph, may sit there and pause ;
All he gets for his praise is the error of times,
 Nurst up by the Pandars of vulgar applause :
 But the gold that is sold
 For Canary, brings wit,
And there is no honour compared to it.

Some love to wear satin and shine in their silk,
 Yet quickly their fashion will alter and vary ;
Sometime they'll eat mutton, sometime they'll drink milk,
 But I am for ever in tune for Canary :
 It is sack that doth make
 All our wants to be nothing,
For we do esteem it both meat, drink, and clothing.

A green goose serves Easter, with gooseberries drest ;
 And July affords us a dish of green peason ;
A collar of brawn is New-year-tide's feast ;
 But sack is for ever and ever in season :
 'Twill suffice all the wise
 Both at all times and places,
It is a good friend to all tempers and cases.

Then farewell metheglin, thou dreg of the hives,
 And cider, thou bastardly darling of summer ;
You dull the quick blood that Canary revives ;
 Then fill me a pottle of sack in a rummer :
 For I'll drink till each chink
 Be full, and 'tis but reason ;
And then I shall have no room to harbour treason.

75

BACCHUS' HEALTH [1]

HERE's a health to jolly Bacchus,
Here's a health to jolly Bacchus,
Here's a health to jolly Bacchus, I-ho, I-ho, I-ho!
For merry he doth make us,
For merry he doth make us,
For merry he doth make us, I-ho, I-ho, I-ho!

Come sit ye down together,
Come sit ye down together,
Come sit ye down together, I-ho, I-ho, I-ho!
And bring more liquor hither,
And bring more liquor hither,
And bring more liquor hither, I-ho, I-ho, I-ho!

It goes into the cranium,
It goes into the cranium,
It goes into the cranium, I-ho, I-ho, I-ho!
And thou'rt a boon companion,
And thou'rt a boon companion,
And thou'rt a boon companion, I-ho, I-ho, I-ho!

Here's a health to jolly Bacchus,
Here's a health to jolly Bacchus,
Here's a health to jolly Bacchus, I-ho, I-ho, I-ho!
For merry he doth make us,
For merry he doth make us,
For merry he doth make us, I-ho, I-ho, I-ho!

[1] From "Pills to Purge Melancholy."

76

A SONG ON BACCHUS [1]

SINCE there's so small difference 'twixt drowning and
    drinking,
We'll tipple and pray, too, like mariners sinking;
Whilst they drink salt water, we'll pledge 'em in wine,
And pay our devotion at Bacchus's shrine :
      Oh ! Bacchus, great Bacchus, for ever defend us,
      And plentiful store of good Burgundy send us.

From censuring the State, and what passes above,
From a surfeit of cabbage, from lawsuits and love,
From meddling with swords and such dangerous things,
And handling of guns in defiance of kings :
      Oh ! Bacchus, etc.

From riding a jade that will start at a feather,
Or ending a journey with loss of much leather ;
From the folly of dying for grief or despair,
With our heads in the water, our heels in the air :
      Oh ! Bacchus, etc.

From an usurer's gripe, and from every man,
That boldly pretends to do more than he can ;
From the scolding of women, and bite of mad dogs,
And wandering over wild Irish bogs :
      Oh ! Bacchus, etc.

[1] From " Pills to Purge Melancholy."

77

A Tankard of Ale

From hunger and thirst, empty bottles and glasses,
From those whose religion consists in grimaces ;
From e'er being cheated by female decoys,
From humouring old men, and reasoning with boys :
   Oh ! Bacchus, etc.

From those little troublesome insects and flies,
That think themselves pretty, or witty, or wise ;
From carrying a quartan for mortification,
As long as a Ratisbon consultation :
      Oh ! Bacchus, great Bacchus, for ever defend us,
      And plentiful store of good Burgundy send us.

A DRINKING SONG

By Henry Carey

BACCHUS must his power resign—
I am the only God of Wine !
It is not fit the wretch should be
In competition set with me,
Who can drink ten times more than he.

Make a new world, ye powers divine !
Stocked with nothing else but wine :
Let wine its only product be,
Let wine be earth, and air, and sea—
And let that wine be all for me.

To Live Merrily, and to Trust to Good Verses

A BACCHANAL[1]

(DUET)

BACCHUS, God of mortal pleasure,
Ever give me of thy treasure.
How I long for t' other quart,
  Ring and call the drowsy waiter
  Hither since it is no later,
Why should good companions part.

Whip a shilling he that's willing,
  Follow this example round.
If you'd wear a lib'ral spirit,
Put about the generous claret,
  After death's no smiling found.

TO LIVE MERRILY, AND TO TRUST TO GOOD VERSES

By ROBERT HERRICK (1591-1674)

Now is the time for mirth,
  Nor cheek or tongue be dumb :
For with the flowery earth,
  The golden pomp is come.

[1] I found this song (which is set to music by Handel) in an untitled volume of songs of the British Museum.

79

A Tankard of Ale

The golden pomp is come ;
　For now each tree doth wear
(Made of her pap and gum)
　Rich beads of amber here.

Now reigns the rose, and now
　Th' Arabian dew besmears
My uncontrolled brow,
　And my retorted hairs.

Homer, this health to thee,
　In sack of such a kind,
That it would make thee see,
　Though thou weit ne'er so blind.

Next, Virgil, I'll call forth,
　To pledge this second health
In wine, whose each cup's worth
　An Indian Commonwealth.

A goblet next I'll drink
　To Ovid ; and suppose,
Made he the pledge, he'd think
　The world had all one nose.

Then this immensive cup
　Of aromatic wine,
Catullus, I quaff up
　To that terse Muse of thine.

To Live Merrily, and to Trust to Good Verses

Wild I am now with heat ;
  O Bacchus ! cool thy rays !
Or frantic I shall eat
  Thy thyrse, and bite the bays.

Round, round, the roof does run ;
  And being ravished thus,
Come, I will drink a tun
  To my Propertius.

Now, to Tibullus, next,
  This flood I drink to thee :
But stay ; I see a text,
  That this presents to me.

Behold, Tibullus lies
  Here burnt, whose small return
Of ashes, scarce suffice
  To fill a little urn.

Trust to good verses then ;
  They only will aspire,
When pyramids, as men,
  Are lost i' th' funeral fire.

And when all bodies meet
  In Lethe to be drown'd ;
Then only numbers sweet
  With endless life are crowned.

A ROUND [1]

BY WILLIAM BROWNE (1590-1645?)

All

Now that the Spring hath fill'd our veins
  With kind and active fire,
And made green liv'ries for the plains,
  And every grove a quire :

— Sing we a song of merry glee,
  And Bacchus fill the bowl.
1. Then here's to thee ; 2. And thou to me,
  And every thirsty soul.

Nor Care nor Sorrow e'er paid debt,
  Nor never shall do mine ;
I have no cradle going yet,
  Not I, by this good wine.

No wife at home to send for me,
  No hogs are in my ground,
No suit in law to pay a fee,
  Then round, old Jocky, round.

All

Shear sheep that have them, cry we still,
  But see that no man 'scape
    To drink of the sherry —
    That makes us so merry,
  And plump as the lusty grape.

[1] From " Songs of the Vine," 1904.

A Catch Royal

HERE'S A HEALTH [1]

BY THOMAS JORDAN (1613–1685)

HERE'S a health unto his Majesty,
 With a fal-la-la-la-la-la-la ;
Confusion to his enemies,
 With a fal-la-la-la-la-la-la.
And he that will not drink his health,
I wish him neither wit nor wealth
Nor yet a rope to hang himself,
 With a fal-la-la-la-la-la-la-la-la !

A CATCH ROYAL

BY THOMAS JORDAN [2]

LET the drawer run down ;
We'll sit and drink the sun down :
 Here's a jolly health to the King !
Let him be confounded
And hanged up for a Roundhead
 That will not pledge me a spring ;
Next to the Lady Mary
This beer-bowl of Canary.
 I'll pledge't a carouse were it ten ;
When Charles his thoughts are eased,
And his great heart appeased,
 We'll drink the sun up again.

[1] From " Merry Drollery."
[2] Text from " Songs of the Vine."

83

DOWN AMONG THE DEAD MEN[1]

By John Dyer (1700–58)

Here's a health to the king and a lasting peace,
To faction an end, to wealth increase ;
Come, let us drink it while we have breath,
For there's no drinking after death.
And he that will this health deny,
Down among the dead men let him lie !

Let charming beauty's health go round,
In whom celestial joys are found,
And may confusion still pursue
The senseless women-hating crew ;
And they that women's health deny,
Down among the dead men let them lie !

In smiling Bacchus' joys I'll roll,
Deny no pleasures to my soul ;
Let Bacchus' health round briskly move,
But Bacchus is a friend to love.
And he that will this health deny,
Down among the dead men let him lie !

May love and wine their rites maintain,
And their united pleasures reign,
While Bacchus' treasure crowns the board,
We'll sing the joys that both afford ;
And they that won't with us comply—
Down among the dead men let them lie !

[1] "Chappell's Collection."

SONG FROM " THE SCHOOL FOR SCANDAL "

By Richard Brinsley Sheridan (1751–1816)

Here's to the maiden of bashful fifteen ;
Here's to the widow of fifty ;
Here's to the flaunting extravagant quean,
And here's to the housewife that's thrifty.

> *Chorus.* Let the toast pass—
> Drink to the lass,
> I'll warrant she'll prove an excuse for a glass.

Here's to the charmer whose dimples we prize ;
Now to the maid who has none, sir ;
Here's to the girl with a pair of blue eyes,
And here's to the nymph with but one, sir.

> *Chorus.* Let the toast pass—
> Drink to the lass,
> I'll warrant she'll prove an excuse for a glass.

Here's to the maid with a bosom of snow ;
Now to her that's as brown as a berry ;
Here's to the wife with a face full of woe,
And now to the damsel that's merry.

> *Chorus.* Let the toast pass—
> Drink to the lass,
> I'll warrant she'll prove an excuse for a glass.

A Tankard of Ale

For let 'em be clumsy, or let 'em be slim,
　Young or ancient, I care not a feather.;
So fill a pint bumper quite up to the brim,
So fill up your glasses, nay, fill to the brim,
　And let us e'en toast them together.

　　Chorus.　Let the toast pass—
　　　　Drink to the lass,
　　I'll warrant she'll prove an excuse for a glass.

ONE BUMPER AT PARTING

By Thomas Moore (1779–1852)

One bumper at parting!—though many
　Have circled the board since we met,
The fullest, the saddest of any,
　Remains to be crowned by us yet.
The sweetness that pleasure has in it
　Is always so slow to come forth,
That seldom, alas! till the minute
　It dies, do we know half its worth!
But fill—may our life's happy measure
　Be all of such moments made up;
They're born on the bosom of pleasure,
　They die 'midst the tears of the cup.

As onward we journey, how pleasant
　To pause and inhabit awhile
Those few sunny spots, like the present,
　That 'mid the dull wilderness smile!
But Time, like a pitiless master,
　Cries " Onward !" and spurs the gay hours ;

86

A Dialogue

And never does Time travel faster
   Than when his way lies among flow'rs.
But come—may our life's happy measure
   Be all of such moments made up ;
They're born on the bosom of pleasure
   They die 'midst the tears of the cup.

This evening we saw the sun sinking
   In waters his glory made bright—
Oh ! trust me, our farewell of drinking
   Should be like that farewell of light.
You saw how he finished by darting
   His beam o'er a deep billow's brim—
So fill up ! let's shine at our parting
   In full liquid glory like him.
And oh ! may our life's happy measure
   Of moments like this be made up ;
'Twas born on the bosom of pleasure,
   It dies 'mid the tears of the cup.

A DIALOGUE [1]

Wine.   I, JOVIAL wine, exhilarate the heart.

Beer.   March beer is a drink for a king.

Ale.   But ale, bonny ale, with spice and a tost,
      In the morning's a dainty thing.

Chorus.   Then let us be merry, wash sorrow away !
      Wine, beer and ale shall be drunk to-day.

[1] 1658. In Garrick Collection.

A Tankard of Ale

Wine.   I, generous wine, am for the court.

Beer.   The citie calls for beer.

Ale.   But ale, bonny ale, like a lord of the soyl,
          In the country shall domineer.

Chours. Then let us be merry, wash sorrow away !
          Wine, beer and ale shall be drunk to-day.

THE EPICURE

By ABRAHAM COWLEY (1618–1667)

FILL the bowl with rosy wine,
Around our temples roses twine,
And let us cheerfully awhile,
Like the wine and roses, smile.
Crown'd with roses, we contemn
Gyges' wealthy diadem.
To-day is ours ; what do we fear ?
To-day is ours ; we have it here.
Let's treat it kindly, that it may
Wish, at least, with us to stay ;
Let's banish business, banish sorrow.
To the gods belongs to-morrow.

DRINK ! DRINK ! THE RED, RED WINE [1]

Drink ! drink ! the red, red wine,
 That in the goblet glows,
Is hallow'd by the blood that stain'd
 The ground whereon it grows.

Drink ! drink ! there's health and joy
 In its foam to the free and brave ;
But 'twould blister up like the elf-king's cup
 The pale lip of the slave !

Drink ! drink ! and as your hearts
 Are warm'd by its ruddy tide,
Swear to live as free as your fathers liv'd,
 Or to die as your fathers died.

A STOOP OF RHENISH

By John Davidson (1837–1909)

When dogs in office frown you down,
And malice smirches your renown ;
When fools and knaves your blunders twit,
And melancholy dries your wit ;
 Be no more dull,
  But polish and plenish
 Your empty skull
  With a stoop of Rhenish.

[1] Set to music as a trio, by Sir H. R. Bishop.

89

A Tankard of Ale

Drink by the card,
    Drink by the score,
Drink by the yard,
    Drink evermore!

When seamy sides begin to show,
And dimples into wrinkles grow;
When care comes in by hook or crook
And settles at your ingle-nook,
    Never disdain
      To polish and plenish
    Your rusty brain
      With a stoop of Rhenish.
Drink by the card,
    Drink by the score,
Drink by the yard,
    Drink evermore!

When hope gets up before the dawn,
And every goose appears a swan;
When time and tide, and chance and fate
Like lackeys on your wishes wait;
    Then fill the bowl,
      And polish and plenish
    Your happy soul
      With a stoop of Rhenish.
Drink by the card,
    Drink by the score,
Drink by the yard,
    Drink evermore!

DRINKING SONG
On the Excellence of Burgundy Wine

BY HILAIRE BELLOC

My jolly fat host with your face all agrin,
Come open the door to us, let us come in.
A score of stout fellows who think it no sin
If they toast till they're hoarse, and they drink till they
  spin.
      Hoofed it amain,
      Rain or no rain,
To crack your old jokes, and your bottles to drain.

Such a warmth in the belly that nectar begets
As soon as his guts with its humour he wets,
The miser his gold, and the student his debts,
And the beggar his rags and his hunger forgets.
      For there's never a wine
      Like this tipple of thine
From the great hill of Nuits to the River of Rhine.

Outside you may hear the great gusts as they go
By Foy, by Duerne and the hills of Lerraulx,
But the rain he may rain, and the wind he may blow,
If the Devil's above there's good liquor below.
      So it abound,
      Pass it around,
Burgundy's Burgundy all the year round.

SONG IN PRAISE OF ALE [1]

Submit, bunch of grapes,
To the strong barley ear;
The weak·wine no longer·
The laurel shall wear.

Sack and all drinks else,
Desist from the strife;
Ale's the only aqua vitæ
And liquor of life.

Then come, my boon fellows,
Let's drink it around;
It keeps us from the grave
Though it lays us on ground.

Ale's a physician,
No mountebank bragger;
Can cure the chill ague,
Though it be with the stagger.

Ale's a strong wrestler,
Flings all it hath met;
And makes the ground slippery,
Though it be not wet.

[1] "London Chanticleer, 1659."

92

In Praise of Ale

Ale is both Ceres,
And good Neptune too,
Ale's froth was the sea
From which Venus grew.

Ale is immortal;
And be there no stops,
In bonny lads quaffing,
Can live without hops.

Then come, my boon fellows,
Let's drink it around;
It keeps us from the grave,
Though it lays us on ground.

IN PRAISE OF ALE [1]

WHEN as the Chilehe Rocko blowes,
And winter tells a heavy tale;
When pyes, and dawes, and rookes, and crowes,
Sit cursing of the frosts and snowes—
Then give me ale.

Ale in Saxon Rumken then,
Such as will make grim Malkin prate;
Rouseth up valour in all men,
Quickens the poet's wit and pen,
Dispiseth fate.

[1] From Merry Drolley. The music for this song is in Ritson's
Collection of English Songs, 1783.

A Tankard of Ale

Ale that the absent battle fights,
 And fames the march of Swedish drums ;
Disputes the princes' lawes and rights,
 And what is past, and what's to come,
  Tells mortal wights.

Ale that the plowman's heart upkeeps,
 And equals it with Tyrants' thrones ;
That wipes the eye that overweepes,
And lulls in sweet and dainty sleepes
  His wearied bones.

Grandchilde of Ceres, Barlie's daughter,
 Wine's emulus neighbour, if but stale ;
Innobling all the nymphs of water,
 And filling each man's heart with laughter —
  Hah ! give me ale !

BRYNG US IN GOOD ALE [1]

Bryng us in good ale, and bryng us in good ale ;
For our blyssyd Lady sak, bryng us in good ale.
Bryng us in no browne bred, fore that is made of brane,
Nor bryng us in no whyt bred, fore therein is no game.
 But bryng us in good ale.

[1] "Songs and Carols of the Fifteenth Century," by Wright.
Percy Society Edition.

Bryng us in Good Ale

Bryng us in no befe, for there is many bonys,
But bryng us in good ale, for that goth down at oyns ;
  And bryng us in good ale.

Bryng us in no bacon, for that is passing fat,
But bryng us in good ale, and gyfe us i-nought of that ;
  And bryng us in good ale.

Bryng us in no mutton, for that is often lene,
Nor bryng us in no trypes, for thei be syldom clene—
  But bryng us in good ale.

Bryng us in no eggys, for there are many schelles,
But bryng us in good ale, and give us nothyng ellys—
  And bryng us in good ale.

Bryng us in no butter, for therein are many herys ;
Nor bryng us in no pygges flesch, for that will make us
    borys—
  But bryng us in good ale.

Bryng us in no podyngès, for therein is al Godes good ;
Nor bryng us in no venesen, for that is not for our blod—
  But bryng us in good ale.

Bryng us in no capon's flesch, for that is ofte der ;
Nor bryng us in no dokes flesch, for thei slober in the
    mer—
  But bryng us in good ale.

A Tankard of Ale

WASSAIL [1]

WASSAIL ! wassail ! all over the toun,
Our toast it is white, and our ale it is broun ;
Our bowl it is made of a Maplin tree ;
We be good fellows all ;—I drink to thee.

Here's to our horse and to his right ear,
God send our measter a happy new year :
A happy new year as e'er he did see—
With my wassailing bowl I drink to thee.

Here's to our mare, and to her right eye,
God send our mistress a good Christmas pie ;
A good Christmas pie as e'er I did see—
With my wassailing bowl I drink to thee.

Here's to our cow, and to her long tail,
God send our measter us never may fail
Of a cup of good beer : I pray you draw near,
And our jolly wassail it's then you shall hear.

Be here any maids ? I suppose here be some ;
Sure they will not let young men stand on the cold
  stone !
Sing hey O, maids ! come trole back the pin,
And the fairest maid in the house let us all in.

[1] Gloucestershire. Tune in " Popular Music."

96

Ballad on Ale

Come, butler, come, bring us a bowl of the best ;
I hope your soul in heaven will rest ;
But if you do bring us a bowl of the small,
Then down fall butler, and bowl and all.

THE NUT-BROWN ALE [1]

By John Marston (1575 ?–1634)

The nut-brown ale, the nut-brown ale,
Puts down all drink when it is stale !
The toast, the nutmeg, and the ginger
Will make a sighing man a singer.
Ale gives a buffet in the head,
  But ginger under-props the brain ;
When ale would strike a strong man dead
  Then nutmeg tempers it again.
The nut-brown ale, the nut-brown ale,
Puts down all drink when it is stale !

BALLAD ON ALE

By John Gay (1685–1732)

While some in epic strains delight,
While others pastorals invite,
  As taste or whim prevail ;
Assist me, all ye tuneful Nine,
Support me in the great design
  To sing of nappy ale.

[1] Published 1610.

A Tankard of Ale

Some folks of cider made a rout,
And cider's well enough, no doubt,
. When better liquors fail ;
But wine, that's richer, better still,
Ev'n wine itself (deny't who will)
  Must yield to nappy ale.

Rum, brandy, gin, with choicest smack,
From Holland brought, Batavia sack,
  All these will nought avail
To cheer a truly British heart,
And lively spirits to impart,
  Like humming, nappy ale.

Oh ! whether thee I closely hug
In honest can or nut-brown jug,
  Or in the tankard hail ;
In barrel or in bottle pent,
I give the generous spirit vent,
  Still may I feast on ale.

But chief when to the cheerful glass,
From vessel pure, thy streamlets pass,
  Then most thy charms prevail ;
Then, then, I'll bet, and take the odds,
That nectar, drink of heathen gods,
  Was poor compared to ale !

Give me a bumper, fill it up :
See how it sparkles in the cup ;
  Oh, how shall I regale ! .

Ballad on Ale

Can any taste this drink divine,
And then compare rum, brandy, wine,
  Or ought with nappy ale?

Inspired by thee the warrior fights,
The lover wooes, the poet writes,
  And pens the pleasing tale;
And still in Britain's isle confest,
Nought animates the patriot's breast
  Like generous, nappy ale.

High church and Low oft raise a strife,
And oft endanger limb and life,
  Each studious to prevail;
Yet Whig and Tory, opposite
In all things else, do both unite
  In praise of nappy ale.

Inspired by thee, shall Crispin sing,
Or talk of freedom, church and king,
  And balance Europe's scale;
While his rich landlord lays out schemes
Of wealth in golden South Sea dreams,
  Th' effects of nappy ale!

O blest potation! still by thee
And thy companion Liberty,
  Do health and mirth prevail;
Then let us crown the can, the glass,
And sportive bid the minutes pass
  In quaffing nappy ale.

A Tankard of Ale

Ev'n while these stanzas I indite,
The bar-bell's grateful sounds invite
  Where joy can never fail.
Adieu, my muse! adieu I haste
To gratify my longing taste
  With copious draughts of ale.

I LIKES A DROP OF GOOD BEER, I DOES [1]

By "Barclay Perkins"

Come, neighbours all, both great and small,
  Let's perform our duties here,
And loudly sing, Long live the King,
  For bating the tax on beer:
  For I likes a little good beer;
And loudly sing, Long live the King,
  For bating the tax on beer.

Some people think distill-e-ry drink
  Is wholesome, neat and sheer,
But I will contend to my life's end,
  There's nothing to tipple like beer:
  For I likes a little good beer;
And I will contend to my life's end,
  There's nothing to tipple like beer.

[1] This admirable song, given in W. T. Marchant's " In Praise
of Ale," was written to celebrate the Act in the reign of William
IV which reduced the duties on ale.

I Likes a Drop of Good Beer, I does.

Brandy and gin blows out the skin,
  And makes one feel very queer :
But whenever I puts them into my stomach
  I always wishes 'twas beer :
  For I likes a little good beer ;
But whenever I puts them into my stomach
  ·I always wishes 'twas beer.

From drinking rum the maggots come,
  And bowel pains appear ;
But I always find both cholic and wind
  Are driven away by beer :
  For I likes a little good beer ;
But I always find that cholic and wind
  Are driven away by beer.

Moll, if I choose, reads out the news
  With voice both firm and clear,
While I eats my tripe, and smokes my pipe,
  And drinks my gallon of beer :
  For I likes a little good beer ;
While I eats my tripe, and smokes my pipe,
  And drinks my gallon of beer.

At the public-house they used to chouse,
  Which caused me many a tear ;
But the new beer shops sell malt and hops,
  And that's the right stuff to make beer :
  For I likes a little good beer ;
But the new beer shops sell malt and hops,
  And that's the right stuff to make beer ;
  For I likes a little good beer

A Tankard of Ale

Of all things thirst I count the worst,
  And always stand in fear;
So when I goes out I carries about
  A little pint bottle of beer:
  For I likes a little good beer;
So when I goes out I carries about
  A little pint bottle of beer;
  For I likes a little good beer.

'Twixt wet and dry I always try
  From the extremes to steer;
And tho' I've shrunk from getting dead drunk,
  I've always been fond of my beer:
  For I likes a little good beer;
And tho' I've shrunk from getting dead drunk,
  I've always been fond of my beer;
  For I likes a little good beer.

Let ministers shape the duty on Cape,
  And ordain that Port shall be dear;
But damn their eyes if ever they tries
  To rob a poor man of his beer;
  For I likes a little good beer;
But damn their eyes if ever they tries
  To rob a poor man of his beer;
  For I likes a drop of good beer.

Beer, Boys, Beer

BEER, BOYS, BEER [1]

(To the tune of "Cheer, boys, cheer !")

BEER ! boys, beer ! no more absurd restriction,
Courage, Bass, Meux and Barclay must give way ;
Half-pints and quarts have vanished like a fiction.
Why, then, submit to the brewers' despot sway ?
Brown stout of England ! much as we may love thee,
(Which by the way, I rather think we do,)
Pale draught of India ! shall they charge us for thee
Twice what you're worth, for the profit of a few ?
Beer ! boys, beer ! abundant, deep and vasty !
Beer ! boys, beer ! the stunning, strong and grand !
Beer ! boys, beer ! the cheap and not the nasty !
Beer ! boys, beer ! at a price a man can stand.

Beer ! boys, beer ! the present scale of prices
Leads to a style of tipple not the best ;
Vile Spanish root, and quassia, which not nice is,
Bad for the bile, and oppressive for the chest.
But let's unite with hearty agitation,
Push for our rights, and battle might and main ;
And ours shall be a large and brimming tankard
Of real wholesome stuff, brewed out of roasted grain.
Beer ! boys, beer ! no more of gentian's nausea ;
Beer ! boys, beer ! with liquorice away ;
Beer ! boys, beer ! no logwood chips or quassia ;
Beer ! boys, beer ! which is all I have to say !

[1] Written in 1855 when a war tax of 1½d. per bushel was im-
posed and the price of beer consequently raised by the brewers
by 6s. per cask. From W. T. Marchant's " In Praise of Ale."

A Tankard of Ale

THE BEER-DRINKING BRITON [1]

YE true, honest Britons, who love your own land,
  Who's sires were so brave, so victorious, so free,
Who always beat France when they took her in hand,
  Come join, honest Britons, in chorus with me.

Join in chorus, join in chorus with me,
Come join, honest Britons, in chorus with me,
Let us sing our own treasures, old England's good cheer,
The profits and pleasures of stout British beer.
Your wine-tippling, dram-sipping fellows retreat,
But your beer-drinking Britons can never be beat.

The French, with their vineyards, are meagre and pale,
  The drink of the squeezings of half-ripened fruit ;
But we, who have hop-grounds to mellow our ale,
  Are rosy and plump and have freedom to boot.
      Let us sing our own treasures, etc.

Should the French dare invade us, thus armed with our
    poles,
  We'll bang their bare ribs, make their lanthorn-jaws
    ring,
, For your beef-eating Britons are valiant souls
  Who will shed their last drop for their country and
    king.
      Let us sing our own treasures, etc.

[1] From "Literary Magazine," May, 1757, where it was
printed with the music.

104

ENGLISH BRIGHT BEER [1]

WHEN humming bright beer was an Englishman's taste,
Our wives they were merry, our daughters were chaste,
Their breath smelt like roses whenever embraced.
   Oh, the bright beer of old England !
   Oh, the old English bright beer !

Ere coffee and tea found the way to the town,
Our ancestors by their own fire sat down ;
Their bread it was white, and their beer it was brown.
   Oh, the brown beer of old England !
   Oh, the old English brown beer !

Our heroes of old, of whose conquests we boast,
Would make a good meal of a pot and a toast ;
This maxim ne'er failed in ruling the roast.
   Oh, the brown-beer, etc.

When the great Spanish fleet on our coast did appear,
Our sailors each one drank a flagon of beer,
And sent them away with a flea in the ear.
   Oh, the bright beer, etc.

Our clergymen then took a cup of good beer,
Ere they mounted the rostrum, their spirits to cheer ;
They preached against vice, although courtiers were near.
   Oh, the bright beer, etc.

[1] From Poole's " Art of Brewing."

Their doctrines were then authentic and bold,
Well grounded on Scripture and fathers of old ;
But now they preach nothing but what they are told.
    Oh, the bright beer, etc.

For since the Geneva and strong ratifie,
We are dwindled to nothing—but stay, let me see
Faith ! nothing at all but mere fiddle-de-dee.
    Oh, the bright beer of old England !
    Oh, the old English bright beer !

A GLASS OF OLD ENGLISH ALE [1]

By J. Caxton

THEY talk about their foreign wines—Champagne and
    bright Moselle,
And think because they're from abroad that we must
    like them well.
And of their wholesome qualities they tell a wondrous
    tale ;
But sour or sweet they cannot beat a glass of old English
    ale.
              Chorus

    So come what will, boys, drink it still
    Your cheeks 'twill never pale.
    Their foreign stuff is well enough,
    But give me old English ale,
      My boys,
    But give me old English ale.

[1] Set to music by Mallardaine and published by Cocks and
Co., New Burlington St. Text from Marchant's " In Praise
of Ale."

Glorious Beer

When schoolboy friends meet once again, who have not
  met for years,
Say over what will they sit down and talk of their careers,
Your " wishy-washy " wines won't do, and fiery spirits
  fail,
For nothing blends the hearts of friends like good old
  English ale.
> *Chorus.* So come what will, etc.

Dy'e think my eye would be as bright, my heart as light
  and gay,
If I and " old John Barleycorn " did not shake hands
  each day ?
No, no ; and though teetotallers at malt and hops may
  rail,
At them I'll laugh and gaily quaff my glass of old English
  ale.
> *Chorus.* So come what will, etc.

GLORIOUS BEER [1]

Beer, beer, glorious beer !
  Fill yourselves right up to here !.
Drink a good deal of it—make a good meal of it,
  Stick to your old fashion'd beer !
Don't be afraid of it—drink till you're made of it—
  Now altogether, a cheer !
Up with the sale of it—down with a pail of it—
  Glorious, glorious beer !

[1] I omit all else but the chorus in a song unworthy of it. The
publishers are Messrs. Day and Hunter.

A Tankard of Ale

ENGLISH ALE [1]

BY WILLIAM HARRISON AINSWORTH (1805–82)

OH, froth me a flagon of English ale,
Stout and old as amber-pale,
Which heart and head will alike assail,
 Ale, ale be mine.

Or brew me a pottle of sturdy sack,
Sherries and spice with a toast at its back,
And need shall be none to bid me attack
 That drink divine.

Or brew me a pottle of sturdy sack,
And need shall be none to bid me attack,
 That drink divine !
 That drink divine !

Still I prefer a flagon of ale, ha ! ha !
Stout and old, ha ! ha ! and as amber pale, ha ! ha !
Which head and heart will alike assail.
 Ale, ale be mine. Ale, ale,
 Fine old English ale, ale, ale,
 Fine old English ale ! Ale be mine !

[1] Set to Music by G. H. Rodwell, and published by Messrs.
J. B. Cramer and Co.

Your Gaul may tipple his thin, thin wine,
And pate of its hue and its fragrance fine,
   Shall never a drop pass throat of mine again.
His claret is meagre, but let that pass ;
I can't say much for his hypocrass,
And never more will I fill my glass
   With cold champaign,
His claret is meagre (but let that pass),
And never more will I fill my glass
With cold, with cold champaign,
   With cold champaign,
For, oh, I prefer a flagon of ale, ha ! ha !
Stout and old, ha ! ha ! and as amber pale, ha ! ha !
Which heart and head will alike assail. Ale, ale be mine
Ale, ale, fine old English ale, ale, ale,
   Fine old English ale be mine.

BEER

By C. S. Calverley (1831–1884)

In those old days which poets say were golden—
   (Perhaps they laid the gilding on themselves :
And if they did, I'm all the more beholden
   To those brown dwellers in my dusty shelves,
Who talk to me " in language quaint and olden "
   Of gods and demigods and fauns and elves,
- Pan with his pipes, and Bacchus with his leopards,
And staid young goddesses who flirt with shepherds :)

A Tankard of Ale

In those old days, the Nymph called Etiquette
  (Appalling thought to dwell on) was not born.
They had their May, but no Mayfair as yet,
  No fashions varying as the hues of morn.
Just as they pleased they dressed and drank and ate,
  Sang hymns to Ceres (their John Barleycorn)
And danced unchaperoned, and laughed unchecked,
And were no doubt extremely incorrect.

Yet do I think their theory was pleasant :
  And oft, I own, my " wayward fancy roams "
Back to those times, so different from the present ;
  When no one smoked cigars, nor gave at-homes,
Nor smote a billiard ball, nor winged a pheasant,
  Nor " did " their hair by means of long-tailed combs,
Nor-migrated to Brighton once a year,
Nor—most astonishing of all—drank Beer.

No, they did not drink Beer, " which brings me to "
  (As Gilpin said) " the middle of my song."
Not that " the middle " is precisely true,
  Or else I should not tax your patience long :
If I had said " beginning," it might do ;
  But I have a dislike to quoting wrong :
I was unlucky—sinned against, not sinning—
When Cowper wrote down " middle " for " beginning."

So to proceed. That abstinence from Malt
  Has always struck me as extremely curious.
The Greek mind must have had some vital fault,
  That they should stick to liquors so injurious—

·110·

Beer

(Wine, water, tempered p'raps with Attic salt)—
   And not invent at once that mild luxurious,
And artful beverage, Beer. How the digestion·
Got on without it, is a startling question.

Had they digestions ? 'And an actual body
   Such as dyspepsia might make attacks on ?
Were they abstract ideas—(Like Tom Noddy
   And Mr. Briggs)—or men like Jones and Jackson ?
Then Nectar—was that beer or whisky-toddy ?
   Some say the Gaelic mixture, *I* the Saxon :
I think a strict adherence to the latter.
Might make some Scots less pig-headed, and fatter.

Besides, Bon Gaultier definitely shows
   That the real beverage for feasting gods on
Is a soft compound, grateful to the nose
   And also to the palate, known as " Hodgson."
I know a man—a tailor's son—who rose
   To be a peer : and this I would lay odds on
(Though in his Memoirs it may not appear)
That that man owed his rise to copious Beer.

Oh Beer ! Oh Hodgson, Guinness, Allsopp, Bass !
   Names that should be on every infant's tongue !
Shall days and months and years and centuries pass,
   And still your merits be unrecked, unsung ?
Oh ! I have looked into my foaming glass,
   And wished that lyre could yet again be strung
Which once rang prophet-like through Greece, and taught
     her
Misguided sons that " the best drink was water."

A Tankard of Ale

How would he now recant that wild opinion,
  And sing—as would that *I* could sing—of you !
I was not born (alas !) the " Muses' minion,"
  I'm not poetical, nor even blue :
And he (we know) but strives with waxen pinion,
  Whoe'er he is that entertains the view
Of emulating Pindar, and will be
Sponsor at last to some now nameless sea.

Oh ! when the green slopes of Arcadia burned
  With all the lustre of the dying day,
And on Cithaeron's brow the reaper turned,
  (Humming of course in his delightful way,
How Lycidas was dead, and how concerned
  The Nymphs were when they saw his lifeless clay ;
And how rock told to rock the dreadful story
That poor young Lycidas was gone to glory :)

What would that lone and labouring soul have given,
  At that soft moment, for a pewter pot ?
How had the mists that dimmed his eye been riven,
  And Lycidas and sorrow all forgot ?
If his own grandmother had died unshriven,
  In two short seconds he'd have recked it not ;
Such power hath Beer. The heart which Grief hath
  cankered
Hath one unfailing remedy—the Tankard !

Coffee is good, and so no doubt is cocoa ;
  Tea did for Johnson and the Chinamen :
When " Dulce est desipere in loco "
  Was written, real Falernian winged the pen.

Beer

When a rapt audience has encored " Fra Poco "
Or " Casta Diva," I have heard that then
The Prima Donna, smiling herself out,
Recruits her flagging powers with bottled stout.

But what is coffee but a noxious berry,
   Born to keep used-up Londoners awake ?
What is Falernian, what is Port or Sherry,
   But vile concoctions to make dull heads ache ?
Nay, stout itself—(though good with oysters, very)—
   Is not a thing your leading man should take.
He that would shine, and petrify his tutor,
   Should drink draught Allsopp in its " native pewter."

But hark ! a sound is stealing on my ear—
   A soft and silvery sound—I know it well.
Its tinkling tells me that a time is near
   Precious to me—it is the Dinner Bell.
Oh blessed Bell ! Thou bringest beef and beer,
   Thou bringest good things more than tongue may tell ;
Seared is (of course) my heart—but unsubdued
Is, and shall be, my appetite for food.

I go, untaught and feeble is my pen :
   But on one statement I may safely venture ;
That few of our most highly gifted men
   Have more appreciation of the trencher.
I go. One pound of British beef, and then
   What Mr. Swiveller called a " modest quencher " ;
That home-returning, I may " soothly say,"
" Fate cannot touch me : I have dined to-day."

CIDER APPLES

By C. W. Dalmon

Some choose to worship in the church;
  Some choose to worship in the chapels;
But we will worship by ourselves
  In orchards full of cider apples.

Who sends their blossom in the Spring?
  Who sets it in the Summer weather?
Who ripens them at Autumn time?
  'Tis Him we'll worship all together!

And they may mock us in the church;
  And they may jeer us in the chapels;
But we will listen unto Him
  Who loads the trees with cider apples.

A CIDER SONG

By G. K. Chesterton

The wine they drink in Paradise
They make in Haute Lorraine;
God brought it burning from the sod
To be a sign and signal rod
That they that drink the blood of God
Shall never thirst again.

Inishowen

The wine they praise in Paradise
They make in Ponterey,
The purple wine of Paradise,
But we have better at the price ;
It's wine they praise in Paradise,
It's cider that they pray.

The wine they want in Paradise
They find in Plodder's End,
The apple wine of Hereford,
Of Hafod Hill and Hereford,
Where woods went down to Hereford,
And there I had a friend.

The soft feet of the blessed go
In the soft western vales,
The road the silent saints accord,
The road from Heaven to Hereford,
Where the apple wood of Hereford
Goes all the way to Wales.

INISHOWEN

By William Maginn (1793–1842)

I CARE not a fig for a flagon of flip
    Or a whistling can of rumbo ;
But my tongue through whisky-punch will slip
    As nimble as Hurlothrumbo.
So put the spirits on the board,
    And give the lemons a squeezer,
And we'll mix a jorum, by the Lord !
    That will make your worship sneeze, sir.

A Tankard of Ale

The French, no doubt, are famous souls,
  I love them for their brandy ;
In rum and sweet tobacco rolls
  Jamaica men are handy.
The big-breeched Dutch in juniper gin,
  I own are very knowing ;
But are rum, gin, brandy worth a pin,
  Compared with Inishowen ?

Though here with a lord 'tis jolly and fine,
  To tumble down Lachryma Christi,
And over a skin of Italy's wine
  To get a little misty.
Yet not the blood of the Bordeaux grape,
  The finest grape juice going,
Nor clammy Constania, the pride of the Cape,
  Prefer I to Inishowen.

RUM AND MILK

By C. W. Dalmon

Now some may drink to ladies fine,
  With painted cheeks and gowns of silk ;
But we will drink to dairymaids,
  In pocket-mugs of rum and milk !
    O, 'tis up in the morning early,
    When the dew is on the grass,
    And St. John's bell rings for matins,
    And St. Mary's rings for mass !

Captain Stratton's Fancy

The merry skylarks soar and sing,
  And seem to Heaven very near—
Who knows what blessed inns they see,
  What holy drinking songs they hear ?
    O, 'tis up in the morning early,
      When the dew is on the grass,
    And St. John's bell rings for matins,
      And St. Mary's rings for mass !

The mushrooms may be priceless pearls
  A queen has lost beside the stream,
But rum is melted rubies when
  It turns the milk to golden cream !
    O, 'tis up in the morning early,
      When the dew is on the grass,
    And St. John's bell rings for matins,
      And St. Mary's ring for mass !

CAPTAIN STRATTON'S FANCY

By John Masefield

Oh some are fond of red wine and some are fond of white,
And some are all for dancing by the pale moonlight ;
But rum alone's the tipple, and the heart's delight
  Of the old, bold mate of Henry Morgan.

Oh some are fond of Spanish wine, and some are fond of
    French,
And some'll swallow tay and stuff fit only for a wench ;
But I'm for right Jamaica till I roll beneath the bench,
  Says the old, bold mate of Henry Morgan.

A Tankard of Ale

Oh some are for the lily, and some are for the rose,
But I am for the sugar-cane that in Jamaica grows;
For it's that makes the bonny drink to warm my copper
    nose,
    Says the old, bold mate of Henry Morgan.

Oh some are fond of fiddles and a song well sung
And some are all for music for to lilt upon the tongue;
But mouths were made for tankards, and for sucking at
    the bung,
    Says the old, bold mate of Henry Morgan.

Oh some are fond of dancing, and some are fond of dice,
And some are all for red lips, and pretty lasses' eyes;
But a right Jamaica puncheon is a finer prize
    To the old, bold mate of Henry Morgan.

Oh some that's good and godly ones they hold that it's a
    sin
To troll the jolly bowl around, and let the dollars spin;
But I'm for toleration and for drinking at an inn,
    Says the old, bold mate of Henry Morgan.

Oh some are sad and wretched folk that go in silken suits
And there's a mort of wicked rogues that live in good
    reputes;
So I'm for drinking honestly, and dying in my boots,
    Like an old, bold mate of Henry Morgan.

THE LEATHER BOTTEL [1]

God above who rules all things,
Monks, and abbots, and beggars and kings,
The ships that on the sea do swim,
The earth and all that is therein.
Not forgetting the old cow's hide ;
And everything else in the world beside ;
For when we've said and done all we can,
'Tis all for the good and use of man.
So I hope his soul in heaven may dwell,
That first devised the leather bottel.

Now what do you say to these cans of wood ?
Oh no, in faith, they cannot be good ;
For if the bearer fall by the way,
Why on the ground your liquor doth lay ;
But had it been a leather bottel,·
Although he had fallen, all-had been well.
     So I hope his soul, etc.

What say ye to these glasses fine ?
Faith ! they shall have no praise of mine ;
For if you touch your glass on the brim,
The liquor falls out and leaves none therein,

[1] There are several versions of this fine song, first published as
a broadside in the seventeenth century (see " Chappell's Collection," " Roxburghe Ballads," " Pills to Purge Melancholy,"
etc.), but the one I give here is a composite of all.

119

A Tankard of Ale

And though your tablecloth be ever so fine,
There lies your beer, your ale, your wine ;
Whereas had it been the leather bottel,
And the stopper been in, it had been well :
    So I hope his soul, etc.

What do you say to these tankards fine ?
Faith ! they shall have no praise of mine !
For when a lord is about to dine,
And sends them to be filled with wine,
The man with the tankard doth run away,
Because it is silver most gallant and gay.
    So I hope his soul, etc.

Then what do you say to these black jacks three ?
Faith they shall have no praise from me ;
For when a man and his wife are at strife,
Which is much too often the case in life,
Why then they seize on the black jack both,
And in the scuffle they spill the broth ;
Not thinking that at a future day
They must account for throwing good liquor away ;
Whereas had it been the leather bottel,
And the stopper been in, they could have banged away
    well.
    So I hope his soul, etc.

A leather bottel we know is good,
Far better than glasses or cans or wood,
For when a man's at work in the field,
Your glasses and pots no comforts will yield

The Leather Bottel

But a good leather bottel standing by,
Will raise his spirits, whenever he's dry.
    So I hope his soul, etc.

At noon the haymakers sit them down,
To drink from their bottels of ale so brown;
In summer, too, when the weather is warm,
A good bottel full will do them no harm.
Then the lads and the lasses begin to tattle,
But what would they do without this bottel.
    So I hope his soul, etc.

There's never a lord, an earl, or knight,
But in this bottel doth take delight;
For when he's hunting of the deer,
He oft doth wish for a bottel of beer.
Likewise the man that works in the wood,
A bottel of beer will oft do him good.
    So I hope, etc.

And when the bottel at last grows old,
And will good liquor no longer hold,
Out of the side you may make a clout,
To mend your shoes when they're worn out;
Or take and hang it up on a pin,
'Twill serve to put your odd trifles in—
So I hope his soul in heaven may dwell
That first devised the leather bottel.

A Tankard of Ale

THERE WAS A POOR SMITH [1]

THERE was a poor smith lived in a poor toun,
That had a loving wife bonny and brown,
And though he were very discreet and wise,
Yet he would do nothing without her advice;
His stock it grew low, full well did he know,
He told his sweet wife what he intended to do,
Quoth he, sweet wife, if I can prevail,
I will shoe horses, and thou shalt sell ale.

I see by my labour but little I thrive
And that against the stream I do strive;
By selling of Ale some money is got,
If every man honestly pays for his pot:
By this we may keep the wolf from the door,
And live in good fashion though now we live poor;
If we have good custom, we shall have quick sale,
So may we live bravely by selling of ale.

Kind husband, quoth she, let be as you said,
It is the best motion that ever you made,
A stan of good Ale let me have in,
A dozen of good white bread in my Bin;

[1] From John Ashton's "Humour, Wit and Satire of the Seventeenth Century." This song was written by Humfrey Crowch, all of whose work was published from 1637 to 1687. To the tune of " Young man, remember delights are but vain."

There was a Poor Smith

Tobacco likewise we must not forget,
Men will call for it when malt's above wheat.
When once it is known, then o'er hill and dale,
Men will come flocking to taste of our ale.

They sent for a wench, her name it was *Besse*,
And her they hired to welcome their guesse,
They took in good Ale, and many things mo,
The Smith had got him two strings to his bow :
Good fellows came in, and gan for to rore,
The Smith he was never so troubled before,
But quoth the good wife, sweet hart do not rayl,
These things must be if we sell Alè.

The Smith went to his work every day,
But still one or other would call him away,
For now he had got him the name of an Host,
It cost him many a pot and a Toste.
Beside much precious time he now lost,
And thus the poor Smith was every day crost,
But quoth the good wife, sweet hart do not rayl,
These things must be if we sell Ale.

Men run on the score, and little they paid,
Which made the poor Smith be greatly dismaied,
And bonny *Besse* though she were not slack
To welcome her guesse, yet things went to wrack ;
For she would exchange a pot for a kisse,
Which any fellow should seldom times misse,
But quoth the good wife, sweet hart do not rayl,
These things must be if we sell Ale.

A Tankard of Ale

The Smith went abroad, at length he came home,
And found his maid and man in a room,
Both drinking together foot to foot,
To speak to them he thought was no boot :
For they were both drunk and could not reply,
To make an excuse as big as a lye.
But quoth the good wife, sweet hart do not rayl,
These things must be if we sell Ale.

He came home again and there he did see
His wife kindly sitting on a man's knee,
And though he said little, yet thought he the more,
And who can blame the poor Wittall therefor.
He hug'd her and kist her though Vulcan stood by,
Which made him to grumble, and look all awry.
But quoth the good wife, sweet hart do not rayl,
These things must be if we sell Ale.

A Sort of Saylers were drinking one night,
And when they were drunk began for to fight,
The Smith came to part them, as some do report,
For his good will was beat in such sort
That he could not lift his arms to his head,
Nor yet very hardly creep up to his bed.
But quoth the good wife, sweet hart do not rayl,
These things must be if we sell Ale.

A flock of good fellows, all Smiths by their trade,
Within a while after a holiday made,
Unto the Smith's house they came then with speed,
And there they were wondrous merry indeed,

Joan's Ale was New

With my pot and thy pot to make the score higher,
Mine Host was so drunk that he fell in the fire.
But quoth the good wife, sweet hart do not rayl,
These things must be if we sell Ale.

But men ran so much with him on the score,
That Vulcan at last grew wondrous poor,
He owed the Brewer and Baker so much,
They thretned to arrest him, his case it was such ;
He went to his Anvill, to my pot and thine,
He turn'd out his Maid, he pull'd down his Signe,
But O (quoth the good wife) why should we fail,
These things should not be if we sell Ale.

The Smith and his boy went to work for some chink,
To pay for the liquor which others did drink.
Of ale trades in London few break as I heare,
That sell Tobacco, strong Ale and good Beer,
They might have done better, but they were loth
To fill up their measure with nothing but froth.
Let no Ale-house keeper at my song rayl,
These things must be if they sell Ale.

JOAN'S ALE WAS NEW [1]

THERE were six jovial tradesmen,
And they all sat down to drinking,
For they were a jovial crew ;
They sat themselves down to be merry;

[1] From Bell's "Poems, Ballads and Songs of the English Peasantry."

A Tankard of Ale

And they called for a bottle of sherry;
You're welcome as the hills, says Nolly,
While Joan's ale is new, brave boys,
   While Joan's ale is new.

The first that came in was a soldier
With his firelock over his shoulder,
Sure no one could be bolder,
   And a long broadsword he drew:
He swore he would fight for England's ground,
Before the nation should be run down;
He boldly drank their healths all round,
   While Joan's ale was new.

The next that came in was a hatter,
Sure no one could be blacker,
And he began to chatter,
   Among the jovial crew:
He threw his hat upon the ground,
And swore every man should spend his pound,
And boldly drank their healths all round,
   While Joan's ale was new.

The next that came in was a dyer,
And he sat himself down by the fire,
For it was his heart's desire
   To drink with the jovial crew:
He told the landlord to his face
The chimney corner should be his place,
And there he'd sit and dye his face,
   While Joan's ale was new.

Joan's Ale was New

The next that came in was a tinker,
And he was no small beer drinker,
And he was no strong ale shrinker
    Among the jovial crew ;
For his brass nails were made of metal,
And he swore he'd go and mend a kettle,
Good heart, how his hammer and nails did rattle,
    While Joan's ale was new.

The next that came in was a tailor
With his bodkin, shears, and thimble,
He swore he would be nimble,
    Among the jovial crew ;
They sat and they called for ale so stout
Till the poor tailor was almost broke,
And was forced to go and pawn his coat,
    While Joan's ale was new.

The next that came in was a ragman,
With his rag-bag over his shoulder,
Sure no one could be bolder,
    Among the jovial crew ;
They sat and, called for pots and glasses
Till they were all as drunk as asses,
And burnt the old ragman's bag to ashes,
    While Joan's ale was new.

A Tankard of Ale

DO NOTHING BUT EAT [1]

By William Shakespeare (1564–1616)

Do nothing but eat, and make good cheer,
And praise God for the merry year;
When flesh is cheap and females dear,
And lusty lads roam here and there,
  So merrily,
  And ever among so merrily.

Be merry, be merry, my wife has all,.
For women are shrews, both short and tall :
'Tis merry in hall when beards wag all,
  And welcome merry Shrove-tide.
    Be merry, be merry, etc.

A cup of wine that's brisk and fine,
And drink unto the leman mine ;
  And a merry heart lives long-a.
Fill the cup and let it come,
I'll pledge you a mile to the bottom.

WITH NEVER A PENNY OF MONEY

Thomas Ravenscroft (1592–1635)

We be souldiers three,
  (*Pardona moy ie vous an pree*)
Lately come forth of the Low Country,
  With never a penny of money.
    Fa la la la lantido dilly.

[1] From Henry IV. Part II. Act v, Sc. iii.

Come, all you Jolly Watermen

Here, good fellow, I drinke to thee,
(*Pardona moy ie vous an pree*)
To all good fellows where ever they be,
With never a penny of money.

And he will not pledge me this,
(*Pardona moy ie vous an pree*)
Payes for the shot whatever it is,
With never a penny of money.

Charge it againe, boy, charge it againe,
(*Pardona moy ie vous an pree*)
As long as there is any incke in my pen,
With never a penny of money.

COME, ALL YOU JOLLY WATERMEN[1]

Come, all you jolly watermen,
  That on the Thames do ply,
Haul up your boats and wet your throats,
  For rowing makes us dry.

The noble prince we've landed
  Has-tipped us store of gold,
Ne'er spare of wealth to drink his health
  So long as our tizzies hold.

---

[1] From a broadsheet in the British Museum. The music may be found in the minstrelsy of England. It celebrates the marriage of the Princess Mary with William of Orange in 1734.

A Tankard of Ale

Here's half is for our landladies,
  And half is for our wives,
In wet or dry where'er we ply
  We all lead jovial lives.

So here's a health to our noble King,
  And our gracious Queen beside,
Also the Prince of Orange,
  And we'll not forget his bride.

Also that trade may flourish,
  And pride may have a fall,
And dear old England hold her head
  As high as the best of all.

THREE MAN SONG [1]

By Thomas Dekker (1570?–1641?)

Cold's the wind, and wet's the rain,
  Saint Hugh be our good speed:
Ill is the weather that bringeth no gain,
  Nor helps good hearts in need.

Trowl the bowl, the jolly nut-brown bowl,
  And here, kind mate, to thee,
Let's sing a dirge for Saint Hugh's soul,
  And down it merrily.

[1] From " The Shoemaker's Holiday."

The Cobblers' Catch

Down a down, hey down a down,
  Hey derry, derry down a down,
Ho, well done, to me let come,
  Ring compass, gentle joy.

Trowl the bowl, the nut-brown bowl,
  And here, kind mate, to thee,
Let's sing a dirge for Saint Hugh's soul,
  And down it merrily.

Cold's the wind, and wet's the rain,
  Saint Hugh be our good speed,
Ill is the weather that bringeth no gain,
  Nor helpeth good hearts in need.

THE COBBLERS' CATCH

By Robert Herrick (1591–1674)

Come sit we by the fireside,
  And roundly drink we here;
Till that we see our cheeks ale-dyed
  And noses tann'd with beer.

131

THE HOP PLANTER'S SONG [1]

OR

DOWN WITH THE FRENCH

COME, my jolly brisk boys, lay your hop-poles aside,
  Each lad take his can and his wench ; —
Old England now sails with the wind and the tide
  To rouse us and down with the French.

What's he that presides at the Court of Versailles,
  To the planter that sits on this Bench.
Huzza ! for your Hops, your stout Beer, and good Ales
  Down with French wine and down with the French.

Inspired by such martial strong liquors as these,
  Our thirst for revenge we will quench.
Our Sovreign, our Sailors, our Ships and our Seas
  Are united to down with the French.

Tho' void of all weapons, of guns and of swords,
  While his fist a brave Briton can clench,
He will sway by the weapons which nature affords,
  'Gainst the cuts and the arms of the French.

Our Ports, like our hearts, shall be open and free,
  We scorn for to fly or entrench :
Take your liquor, my Bucks, take your liquor with glee,
  Down with that and then down with the French.

[1] From an untitled collection of eighteenth-century drinking songs in the British Museum.

THE CHURN SUPPER [1]

God rest you, merry gentlemen !
Be not moved at my strain,
For nothing study shall my brain,
    But for to make you laugh :
For I come here to this feast,
For to laugh, carouse, and jest,
And welcome shall be every guest,
    To take his cup and quaff.

Chorus

Be frolicsome, every one,
Melancholy none ;
Drink about !
Let it out,
And then we'll all go home,
And then we'll all go home.

This ale is a gallant thing,
It cheers the spirits of a king,
It makes a dumb man strive to sing,
    Aye, and a beggar play !
A cripple that is lame and halt,
And scarce a mile a day can walk,
When he feels the juice of malt,
    Will throw his crutch away.

Chorus.   Be frolicsome, etc.

[1] From Robert Bell's "Early Songs and Ballads," 1885. George Bell and Sons.

A Tankard of Ale

'Twill make the parson forget his men,
'Twill make the clerk forget his pen,
'Twill turn a tailor's giddy brain,
    And make him break his wand.
The blacksmith loves it as his life,
It makes the tinker bang his wife,
Aye, and the butcher seek his knife
    When he has it in his hand !
        Chorus. Be frolicsome, etc.

So now to conclude, my merry boys all,
Let's with strong liquor take a fall,
Although the weakest goes to the wall,
    The best is but a play !
For water it concludes in noise,
Good ale will cheer our hearts, brave boys ;
Then put it round with cheerful voice,
    We meet not every day.
        Chorus. Be frolicsome, etc.

THE COUNTRY FARMER'S VAIN GLORY [1]

Our oats they are hoed, and our barley's reap'd,
Our hay it is mow'd, and our hovel's heap'd :
    Harvest home, harvest home !
We'll merrily roar our harvest home !
    Harvest home ! harvest home !
We'll merrily roar our harvest home !

[1] From the Roxburghe Ballads.

134

The Barley Mow

We cheated the parson, we'll cheat him again ;
For why should the vicar have one in ten,
   One in ten, one in ten,
For why should the vicar have one in ten ?

For staying while dinner is cold and hot
And pudding and dumplings burnt to pot,
   Burnt to pot, burnt to pot,
Till pudding and dumpling's burnt to pot.

We'll drink off our liquor while we can stand,
And hey for the honour of old England,
   Old England, old England,
And hey for the honour of old England !

THE BARLEY MOW [1]

Here's a health to the barley-mow, my brave boys,
   Here's a health to the barley-mow !
We'll drink it out of the jolly brown bowl,
   Here's a health to the barley mow !
Chorus. Here's a health to the barley-mow, my brave
      boys,
     Here's a health to the barley-mow !

[1] A traditional Cornish and Devonshire song, sung on completing the carrying home of the barley. Published in Chappell's "Popular Music."

A Tankard of Ale

We'll drink it out of the nipperkin, boys,
Here's a health to the barley-mow !
The nipperkin and the jolly brown bowl,
    Chorus. Here's a health, etc.

We'll drink it out of the quarter-pint, boys,
Here's a health to the barley-mow !
The quarter-pint, nipperkin and the jolly brown
    bowl,
    Chorus. Here's a health, etc.

We'll drink it out of the half a pint, boys,
Here's a health to the barley-mow !
The half a pint, quarter-pint, etc.
    Chorus. Here's a health, etc.

We'll drink it out of the pint, my brave boys,
Here's a health to the barley-mow !
The pint, the half a pint, etc.
    Chorus. Here's a health, etc.

We'll drink it out of the quart, my brave boys,
Here's a health to the barley-mow !
The quart, the pint, etc.
    Chorus. Here's a health, etc.

We'll drink it out of the pottle, my boys,
Here's a health to the barley-mow !
The pottle, the quart, etc.
    Chorus. Here's a health, etc.

The Barley Mow

We'll drink it out of the gallon, my boys,
  Here's a health to the barley-mow !
The gallon, the pottle, etc.

    Chorus. Here's a health, etc.

We'll drink it out of the half-anker, boys,
  Here's a health to the barley-mow !
The half-anker, gallon, etc.

    Chorus. Here's a health, etc.

We'll drink it out of the anker, my boys,
  Here's a health to the barley-mow !
The anker, the half-anker, etc.

    Chorus. Here's a health, etc.

We'll drink it out of the half-hogshead, boys,
  Here's a health to the barley-mow !
The half-hogshead, anker, etc.

    Chorus. Here's a health, etc.

We'll drink it out of the hogshead, my boys,
  Here's a health to the barley-mow !
The hogshead, the half-hogshead, etc.

    Chorus. Here's a health, etc.

We'll drink it out of the pipe, my brave boys,
  Here's a health to the barley-mow !
The pipe, the hogshead, etc.

    Chorus. Here's a health, etc.

137

A Tankard of Ale

We'll drink it out of the well, my brave boys,
  Here's a health to the barley-mow!
The well, the pipe, etc.

    Chorus. Here's a health, etc.

We'll drink it out of the river, my boys,
  Here's a health to the barley-mow!
The river, the well, etc.

    Chorus. Here's a health, etc.

We'll drink it out of the ocean, my boys,
  Here's a health to the barley-mow!
The ocean, the river, the well, the pipe, the hogshead,
  the half-hogshead, the anker, the half-anker, the
  gallon, the half-gallon, the pottle, the quart, the
  pint, the half a pint, the quarter-pint, the nipperkin,
  and the jolly brown bowl.

Chorus: Here's a health to the barley-mow, my brave
      boys!
     Here's a health to the barley-mow!

HARVEST SONGS [1]

The Master's Health

HERE's a health unto our Master, the founder of the feast,
We wish with all our hearts, sirs, his soul in heaven may
rest ;
That all his works may prosper, whatever he takes in hand,
For we all his servants, and all at his command.
Then drink, boys, drink ! and see you do not spill,
For if you do you shall drink two,
It is our master's will.

The Mistress's Health

This is our mistress's health, merrily singing,
Bonfires in every town, and the bells ringing ;
Cannons are roaring, bullets are flying,
Spaniards away they ran for fear of dying.

[1] From Sawyer's " Sussex Songs and Music." There is a
charming description of the old Sussex manner of singing in
Thomas Geering's " Our Parish." " Master Simmond's prepara-
tion never varied. First he had to twist himself away from the
table, next to pull with both his hands his somewhat long and
new round frock well above his knees, throw the left leg over
the right, stroke his hair straight as he could down over the
forehead, put his pipe between the middle finger of the left
hand, give vent to two or three ahems and haws to clear, as he
said, the passage of the *wine*-pipe, and off he would go, his strong
lungs pulling him through all difficulties of rhyme or rhythm.
His memory never failed him, and he was insistent upon the
recurring chorus ; his eyes were shut, and he never looked
once for light. He was there in his glory ; his light shone full
within him."

A Tankard of Ale

I would·have pleasur'd you had there been fountains,
I would have pleasur'd you had there been mountains;
We'll drink the ocean dry, sack and canary,
This is our mistress's health, drink and be merry.

SAINT GILES'S BOWL

BY WILLIAM HARRISON AINSWORTH (1805–82)

WHERE Saint Giles's Church stands, once a lazar-house
  stood;
And chained to its gates was a vessel of wood;
A broad-bottomed bowl, from which all the fine fellows,
Who passed by that spot on their way to the gallows,
     Might tipple strong beer
     Their spirits to cheer,
  · And drown in a sea of good liquor all fear!
  For·nothing the transit to Tyburn beguiles
  So well as a draught from the Bowl of Saint Giles!

By many a highwayman many a draught
Of nutty-brown ale at Saint Giles's was quaft,
Until the old·lazar-house chanced to fall down,
And the broad-bottomed bowl was removed to the Crown
     Where the robber may cheer
     His spirits with beer
  And drown in a sea of good liquor all fear!
  For nothing the transit to Tyburn beguiles,
  So well as a draught from the Bowl of Saint Giles!

St. Giles's Bowl

There Mulsack and Swiftneck, both prigs from their
  birth,
Old Mob and Tom Cox took their last draught on earth ;
There Randal, and Shorter, and Witney pulled up,
And Jolly Jack Joyce drank his finishing cup !
        For a can of ale calms
        A highwayman's qualms,
    And makes him sing blithely his dolorous psalms !
    For nothing the transit to Tyburn beguiles
    So well as a draught from the Bowl of Saint Giles !

When gallant Jack Sheppard to Tyburn was led,
" Stop the cart at the Crown—stop a moment," he said.,
He was offered the Bowl, but he left it and smiled,
Crying, " Keep it till called for by Jonathan Wild !
        The rascal one day
        Will pass by this way,
    And drink a full measure to moisten his clay !
    And never will Bowl of Saint Giles have beguiled
    Such a thorough-paced scoundrel as Jonathan Wild!"

Should it e'er be my lot to ride backwards that way,
At the door of the Crown I will certainly stay ;
I'll summon the landlord—I'll call for the Bowl,
And drink a deep draught for the health of my soul !
        Whatever may hap,
        I'll taste of the tap,
    To keep up my spirits when brought to the crap !
    For nothing the transit to Tyburn beguiles
    So well as a draught from the Bowl of Saint Giles !

A Tankard of Ale

FROM "NEW YEAR'S DAY"[1]

BY JOHN DAVIDSON (1837–1909)

BASIL

SING hey for the journalist !
He is your true soldado ;
Both time and chance he'll lead a dance,
And find out Eldorado.

BRIAN

Sing hey for Eldorado !

BASIL

A catch, a catch, we'll trowl !

BRIAN

Sing hey for Eldorado !

SANDY

And bring a mazer bowl,
With ale a-frothing brimmed.

BRIAN

We may not rest without it.

SANDY

With dainty ribbons trimmed,
And love-birds carved about it.

[1] Fleet Street Eclogues.

142

From "New Year's Day"

BASIL

With roasted apples scented,
And spiced with cloves and mace.

BRIAN

Praise him who ale invented!

SANDY

In heaven he has a place!

BASIL

Such a comarado
Heaven's hostel never missed!

BRIAN

Sing hey for Eldorado!

SANDY

Sing ho for the journalist!

BASIL

We drink them and we sing them
In mighty humming ale.

BRIAN

May fate together bring them!

A Tankard of Ale

SANDY

Amen !

BASIL

Wass hael !

BRIAN

Drinc häel !

THE MONKS OF THE SCREW

By JOHN PHILPOT CURRAN (1750–1817)

WHEN St. Patrick this order established,
  He called us the " Monks of the Screw ! "
Good rules he revealed to our abbot,
  To guide us in what we should do.
But first he replenished our fountain
  With liquor the best from on high,
And he said, on the word of a saint,
  That the fountain should never run dry.

" Each year, when your octaves approach
  In full chapter convened let me find you ;
And when to the convent you come,
  Leave your favourite temptation behind you.
And be not a glass in your convent—
  Unless on a festival—found ;
And, this rule to enforce, I ordain it
  One festival all the year round.

" My brethren be chaste—till you're tempted ;
  While sober be grave and discreet ;
And humble your bodies with fasting—
  As oft as you've nothing to eat.

144

Friar's Song

Yet in honour of fasting, one lean face
   Among you I'd always require ;
If the abbot should please, he may wear it,
   If not, let it comé to the prior."

Come, let each take his chalice, my brethren,
   And with due devotion prepare,
With hands and with voices uplifted
   Our hymn to conclude with a prayer.
May this chapter oft joyously meet,
   And this gladsome libation renew,
To the saint, and the founder, and abbot,
   The prior, and monks of the Screw !

FRIAR'S SONG

BY WILLIAM MAKEPEACE THACKERAY (1811–63)

SOME love the matin-chimes, which tell
   The hour of prayer to sinner ;
But better far's the midday bell,
   Which speaks the hour of dinner ;
For when I see a smoking fish,
   Or capon drowned in gravy,
Or noble haunch on silver dish,
   Full glad I sing my Ave.

My pulpit is an alehouse bench,
   Whereon I sit so jolly ;
A smiling rosy country wench,
   My saint and patron holy.

A Tankard of Ale

I kiss her cheek so red and sleek,
  I press her ringlets wavy,
And in her willing ear I speak,
  A most religious 'Ave.

And if I'm blind, yet Heaven is kind,
  And holy saints forgiving;
For sure he leads a right good life,
  Who thus admires good living.
Above, they say, our flesh is air,
  Our blood celestial ichor:
Oh, grant! 'mid all the changes there,
  They may not change our liquor!

THE GHOSTS [1]

By Thomas Love Peacock (1785–1866)

In life three ghostly friars were we,
And now three friarly ghosts we be,
  Around our shadowy table placed,
The spectral bowl before us floats :
  With wine that none but ghosts can taste,
We wash our unsubstantial throats.
Three merry ghosts—three merry ghosts—three merry
  ghosts are we :
Let the ocean be Port, and we'll think it good sport
To be laid in that Red Sea !

[1] From " Melincourt."

146

With songs that jovial spectres chaunt,
Our old refectory still we haunt.
 The traveller hears our midnight mirth :
"O list ! " he cries, " the haunted choir !
 The merriest ghost that walks the earth,
Is sure the ghost of a ghostly friar."
Three merry ghosts—three merry ghosts—three merry
     ghosts are we :
Let the ocean be Port, and we'll think it good sport
To be laid in that Red Sea !

THE FRIAR [1]

By Owen Jones (1809–1874 ?)

A JOLLY fat friar loved liquor good store,
 And he had drunk stoutly at supper ;
He mounted his horse in the night at the door,
 And sat with his face to the crupper.
" Some rogue," quoth the friar, " quite dead to remorse,
 Some thief, whom a halter will throttle,
Some scoundrel has cut off the head of my horse,
 While I was engaged with the bottle,
  Which goes gluggity, gluggity, glug."

The tail of his steed pointed south on the vale,
 'Twas the friar's road home, straight and level.
But when spurred, a horse follows his nose, not his tail,
 So he scampered due north like the devil.

[1] Set to music by G. Herbert Rodwell. Published by B.
Williams, 11 Paternoster Row.

A Tankard of Ale

"This new mode of docking," the fat friar said,
  "I perceive does not make a horse trot ill;
And 'tis cheap, for he never can eat off his head,
    While I am engaged with the bottle.
      Which goes gluggity, gluggity, glug."

The steed made a stop, in the pond he had got,
    He was rather for drinking than grazing;
Quoth the friar, "'Tis strange headless horses should trot,
    But to drink with their tail is amazing."
Turning round to find whence this phenomenon arose,
    In the pond fell this son of the bottle;
Quoth he, "The head's found, for I'm under his nose;
    I wish I was over the bottle!
      Which goes gluggity, gluggity, glug."

COMMANDERS OF THE FAITHFUL

By WILLIAM MAKEPEACE THACKERAY (1811–63)

        THE Pope he is a happy man,
      His Palace is the Vatican,
        And there he sits and drains his can:
        The Pope he is a happy man.
      I often say when I'm at home
      I'd like to be the Pope of Rome.

        And then there's Sultan Saladin,
        That Turkish Sultan full of sin;
        He has a hundred wives at least,
        By which his pleasure is increased:

The Little Vagabond

I've often wished, I hope no sin,
That I were Sultan Saladin.

But no, the Pope no wife may choose,
And so I would not wear his shoes ;
No wine may drink the proud Paynim,
And so I'd rather not be him :
My wife, my wine, I love, I hope,
And would be neither Turk nor Pope.

THE LITTLE VAGABOND [1]

BY WILLIAM BLAKE (1757–1827)

DEAR mother, dear mother, the Church is cold ;
But the Alehouse is healthy and pleasant and warm.
Besides I can tell where I am used well ;
The poor parsons with wind like a blown bladder swell.

But if at the Church they would give us some ale,
And a pleasant fire our souls to regale,
We'd sing and we'd pray all the livelong day,
Nor ever once wish from the Church to stray.

Then the Parson might preach and drink and sing,
And we'd be as happy as birds in the spring ;
And modest Dame Lurch, who is always at Church,
Would not have bandy children nor fasting nor birch.

[1] From " Songs of Experience."

149

A Tankard of Ale

And God, like a father, rejoicing to see,
His children as pleasant and happy as he,
Would have no more quarrel with the Devil or the barrel
But kiss him and give him both drink and apparel.

DRINK TO ME ONLY WITH THINE EYES

By Ben Jonson (1573–1637)

Drink to me only with thine eyes,
  And I will pledge with mine;
Or leave a kiss but in the cup,
  And I'll not look for wine.
The thirst that from the soul doth rise,
  Doth ask a drink divine;
But might I of Jove's nectar sip,
  I would not change for thine.

I sent thee, late, a rosy wreath,
  Not so much honouring thee,
As giving it a hope that there
  It could not withered be:
But thou thereon didst only breathe,
  And sent'st it back to me;
Since when, it grows, and smells, I swear,
  Not of itself, but thee!

THE TOPER

BY TOM D'URFEY (1653–1723)

SHE tells me with claret she cannot agree,
And she thinks of a hogshead whene'er she sees me;
For I smell like a beast, and therefor must I
Resolve to forsake her or claret deny :
Must I leave my dear bottle that was always my friend,
And I hope will continue so to my life's end ?
Must I leave it for her ? 'tis a very hard task,—
Let her go to the Devil, bring the other whole flask !

Had she tax'd me with gaming and bade me forbear,
'Tis a thousand to one I had lent her an ear ;
Had she found out my Chloris up three pairs of stairs,
I had baulk'd her and gone to St. James's to pray'rs ;
Had she bid me read homilies three times a day,
She perhaps had been humour'd with little to say ;
But at night to deny me my flask of dear red—
Let her go to the Devil, and there's no more to be said.

THE JOLLY TOPER[1]

THE women all tell me I'm false to my lass,
That I quit my poor Chloe and stick to my glass :
But to you men of Reason, my reasons I'll own,
And if you don't like them why let them alone.

[1] I don't know who wrote this fine song, which I found in an untitled collection of drinking songs of the eighteenth century in the British Museum.

A Tankard of Ale

Altho' I have left her, the truth I'll declare,
I believe she was good, and I'm sure she was fair ;
But goodness and charms in a bumper I see,
That makes it as good and as charming as she.

My Chloe had dimples and smiles I must own,
But tho' she could smile, yet in truth she could frown ;
But tell me, ye lovers of liquor divine,
Did you e'er see a frown in a bumper of wine ?

Her lilies and roses were just in their prime,
Yet lilies and roses are conquered by Time ;
But in wine from its age such a benefit flows,
That we like it the better the older it grows.

They tell me my love would in time have been cloy'd,
And that Beauty's insipid when once 'tis enjoyed :
But in wine I both Time and enjoyment defy,
For the longer I drink the more thirsty am I.

Let murders and battles and history prove
The mischiefs that wait upon rivals in love ;
But in drinking (thank Heaven !) no rival contends,
For the more we love liquor the more we are friends.

She too might have poisoned the joy of my life,
With nurses and babies and squalling and strife ;
But Wine neither nurses nor babies can bring,
And a big-bellied bottle's a mighty good thing.

Now I'm Resolved to Love No More

We shorten our days when with love we engage,
It brings on diseases and hastens old age :
But Wine from grim Death can its votaries save,
And keep out t'other leg, when there's one in the grave.

Perhaps, like her sex, ever false to their word,
She had left me to get an estate or a lord ;
But my Bumper, regarding nor titles nor pelf,
Will stand by me while I can't stand by myself.

Then let my dear Chloe no longer complain,
She's rid of her lover, and I of my pain :
For in wine, mighty wine, my comforts I spy,
Should you doubt what I say, take a bumper and try !

NOW I'M RESOLVED TO LOVE NO MORE [1]

By Alexander Brome (1620–1666)

Now I'm resolv'd to love no more,
  But sleep by night, and drink by day ;
Your coyness, Chloris, pray give o'er,
  And turn your tempting eyes away.
From ladies I'll withdraw my heart,
And fix it only on the quart.

[1] Published 1668.

153

A Tankard of Ale

I'll place no happiness of mine
    A puling beauty still to court,
And say she's glorious and divine—
    The vintner makes the better sport ;
And when I say, my dear, my heart,
I only mean it to the quart.

Love has no more prerogative
    To make me desperate courses take,
Nor me t'an hermitage shall drive,
    I'll all my vows to th' goblet make ;
And if I wear a capuchoone,
It shall a tankard be or none.

'Tis wine alone that cheers the soul,
    But love and ladies make us sad ;
I'm merry when I court the bowl,
    While he who courts the madam's mad ;
Then ladies wonder not at me,
For you are coy but wine is free.

IN PRAISE OF THE BOTTLE [1]

By Tom Brown (1663–1704)

What a plague d'ye tell me of the Papists' design ?
Would to God you'd leave talking, and drink off your
  wine.
Away with your glass, sir, and drown all debate,
Let's be loyally merry, ne'er think of the state.

[1] From W. T. Marchant's " In Praise of Ale."

In Praise of the Bottle

The king (Heaven bless him) knows best how to rule,
And who troubles his head, I think, is but a fool.

Come, sir, here's his health, your brimmer advance,
We'll ingross all the claret, and leave none for France;
'Tis by this we declare our loyal intent,
And by our carousing the customs augment.
Would all mind their drinking, and proper vocation,
We should ha' none of this bustle and stir in the nation.

Let the hero of Poland and monarch of France
Strive, by methods of fighting, their crowns to advance;
Let chapels in Lime Street be built or destroy'd,
And the test and the oath of supremacy void;
It shall ne'er trouble me, I'm none of those maggots,
That have whimsical fancies of Smithfield and faggots.

Then banish all groundless suspicions away,
The king knows to govern, let us learn to obey;
Let every man mind his business and drinking,
When the head's full of wine there's no room left for
    thinking.
'Tis nought but an empty and whimsical pate,
That makes fools run giddy with notions of state.

SONG OF A FALLEN ANGEL OVER A BOWL OF RUM-PUNCH [1]

BY JOHN WILSON ("CHRISTOPHER NORTH")
(1785–1854)

HEAP on more coal there,
  And keep the glass moving,
The frost nips my nose,
  Though my heart glows with loving.
Here's the dear creature,
  No skylights—a bumper ;
He who leaves heeltaps
  I vote him a mumper.
      With hey cow rumble O,
      Whack ! populorum,
      Merrily, merrily men,
      Push round the jorum.

What are Heaven's pleasures
  That so very sweet are ?
Singing from psalters,
  In short or long metre.
Planked on a wet cloud,
  Without any breeches,
Just like the Celtic,
  Met to make speeches.
      With hey cow rumble O, etc.

[1] From " Noctes Ambrosianae."

Song of the Pelagian Heresy

Wide is the difference,
  My own boosing bullies,
Here the round punch-bowl
  Heaped to the full is.
Then if some wise one
  Thinks that up " yonder "
Is pleasant as we are,
  Why—he's in a blunder.
    With hey cow rumble O,
    Whack ! populorum,
    Merrily, merrily men,
    Push round the jorum.

SONG OF THE PELAGIAN HERESY [1]

By Hilaire Belloc

Pelagius lived in Kardanoel,
  And taught his doctrine there :
How whether you went to heaven or hell,
  It was your own affair ;
How whether you rose to eternal joy,
  Or sank forever to burn,
It had nothing to do with the church, my boy,
  But was your own concern.

[1] From " The Four Men."

A Tankard of Ale

Semi-Chorus

Oh, he didn't believe in Adam or Eve—
He put no faith therein ;
His doubts began with the fall of man,
And he laughed at original sin.

Chorus

With my row-ti-dow-ti-oodly-ow,
He laughed at original sin.

Whereat the Bishop of old Auxerre—
Germanus was his name—
He tore great handfuls out of his hair,
And called Pelagius shame.
And then with his stout episcopal staff
So thoroughly thwacked and banged
The heretics all, both short and tall,
That they rather had been hanged.

Semi-Chorus

Oh, he thwacked them hard and he thwacked them
long
On each and all occasions,
Till they bellowed in chorus loud and strong
Their orthodox persuasions.

Chorus

With my row-ti-dow-ti-oodly-ow,
Their orthodox persuasions.

Wine and Water

Now the Faith is old and the Devil is bold—
   Exceeding bold indeed ;
And the masses of doubt that are floating about
   Would smother a mortal creed.
But we who sit in a sturdy youth
   And still can drink strong ale—
Let us put it away to infallible truth
   That always shall prevail.

Semi-Chorus

So thank the Lord for the temporal sword,
   And for howling heretics, too,
And for all the good things that our Christendom
   brings—
   But especially barley brew !

Chorus

With my row-ti-dow-ti-oodly-ow,
   Especially barley brew !

WINE AND WATER[1]

By G. K. Chesterton

Old Noah he had an ostrich farm and fowls on the largest
   scale,
He ate his egg with a ladle in an egg-cup big as a pail,
And the soup he took was Elephant Soup, and the fish he
   took was Whale,
But they all were small to the cellar he took when he set
   out to sail.

[1] From " The Flying Inn."

159

A Tankard of Ale

And Noah he often said to his wife when he sat down to
  dine,
" I don't care where the water goes if it doesn't get into
  the wine."

The cataract of the cliff of heaven fell blinding off the
  brink
As if it would wash the stars away as suds go down a sink;
The seven heavens came roaring down for the throats of
  hell to drink,
And Noah he cocked his eye and said, " It looks like rain,
  I think.
The water has drowned the Matterhorn as deep as a
  Mendip mine,
But I don't care where the water goes if it doesn't get
  into the wine."

But Noah he sinned, and we have sinned ; on tipsy feet
  we trod,
Till a great big black teetotaller was sent to us for a rod,
And you can't get wine at a P.S.A., or chapel, or Eisedd-
  fod,
For the Curse of Water has come again because of the
  wrath of God ;
And water is on the Bishop's board and the Higher
  Thinker's shrine,
But I don't care where the water goes if it doesn't get
  into the wine.

THE ROLLING ENGLISH ROAD[1]

By G. K. Chesterton

BEFORE the Roman came to Rye or out to Severn strode,
The rolling English drunkard made the rolling English
  road.
A reeling road, a rolling road that rambles round the shire,
And after him the parson ran, the sexton and the squire
A merry road, a mazy road, and such as we did tread
The night we went to Birmingham by way of Beachy
  Head.

I knew no harm of Bonaparte and plenty of the Squire,
And for to fight the Frenchman I did not much desire,
But I did bash their baggonets because they came arrayed
To straighten out the crooked road an English drunkard
  made,
Where you and I went down the lane with ale mugs in
  our hands
The night we went to Glastonbury by way of Goodwin
  Sands.

His sins they were forgiven him ; or why do flowers run
Behind him ; and the hedges all strengthening in the sun?
The wild thing went from left to right and knew not
  which was which,
But the wild rose was above him when they found him
  in the ditch.

[1] From " The Flying Inn."

A Tankard of Ale

God pardon us nor harden us; we did not see so clear
The night we went to Bannockburn by way of Brighton
  Pier.

My friends, we will not go again or ape an ancient rage,
Or stretch the folly of our youth to be the shame of age,
But walk with clearer eyes and ears this path that wan-
    dereth,
And see undrugged in evening light the decent inn of
  · death;
For there is good news yet to hear and fine things to be
  - seen,
Before we go to Paradise by way of Kensal Green.

A (TEMPERANCE) DRINKING SONG

By Geoffrey Howard

LANDLORD, I mean to sing to-night;
  To-night I mean to sing.
But bring no wine, nor red, nor white,
  Nor no such filthy thing.
To sit in an inn, and soak with gin,
  Is hateful to my mind;
The glass I clink is crowned with drink
  Of a purely temperance kind.

162

A (Temperance) Drinking Song

Chorus

With drink of a temperance kind, my lads,
  My foaming cup is crowned.
So uncork the Bovril, Landlord, dear,
  And pass the Cocoa round
    And round,
  And pass the Cocoa round !

You Poets of a drunken Muse,
  Are men of little note.
You have to booze and booze and booze,
  To get your wits afloat.
Of Christian beer and right good cheer
  You make a great parade. .
But I can bawl above you all
  On gassy Gingerade !

Chorus

On gassy Gingerade, my sons,
  A beverage light and sound,
So decanter the Lime-juice, Landlord, dear,
  And trot the Kola round
    And round,
  And trot the Kola round !

Milton and Homer both were bards
  Of a highly tedious kind ;
For why ? because these selfsame cards
  For half their lives were blind.

A Tankard of Ale

But Byron, who declared-that wines
  With him did disagree,
Could write the most astounding lines
  On stinking fish and Tea.

Chorus

On stinking fish and Tea, my boys,
  (At one and nine the pound),
So, Landlord, get the Kippers cooked,
  And rush the teapot round
    And round,
  And rush the teapot round !

Marlowe and Shakespeare won renown
  As Poets, it is true ;
And at the " Mermaid " would sit down
  To beef and barley brew ;
But Shaw eats cake and shies at ales,
  And his plays are just as good.
And Garvice writes his serial tales
  On purely cereal food.

Chorus

He lives on cereal food, my friends,
  And so does Ezra Pound.
So, Landlord, open the Plasmon tin,
  And pass the Nutto round
    And round,
  And pass the Nutto round !

A Song of Time's Meridian

But I've one more proof, and a better one still;
  For the most conclusive sign
That in order to sing you need not swill,
  Are these here lines of mine.
My songs, while men shall see the sun,
  With wonder they'll review;
And the best of it is that the whole thing's done
  On Mineral Waters, too.

Chorus

On Ginger-pop I sing until I drop
  And flounder on the ground.
So, Landlord, carry me out with care,
  For your inn is turning round
    And round,
  Your inn is turning round!

A SONG OF TIME'S MERIDIAN

By T. Michael Pope

'Tis half-past six. With eager stride
We haste to where the roads divide.
O hour with joy and gladness fraught!
O pinnacle of Time! Methought
A voice *without* the tavern cried,
        " 'Tis half-past six!"

No longer need we be denied. . . .
The old church clock has surely lied?
Our labour has not been for naught?
      'Tis half-past six?

A Tankard of Ale

A moment we impatient bide. . . . .
Listen ! A welcome stir inside !
What boon the kindly Fates have wrought
For thirsty men awhile distraught ! . . .
The tavern door stands open wide.
                    'Tis half-past six !

DRINKING SONG

By THEODORE MAYNARD

WHEN Horace wrote his noble verse,
  His brilliant, glowing line,
He must have gone to bed the worse
  For good Falernian wine.
No poet yet could praise the rose
In verse that so serenely flows
Unless he dipped his Roman nose
  In good Falernian wine.

Shakespeare and Jonson too
Drank deep of barley brew—
Drank deep of barley brew, my boys,
Drank deep of barley brew !

When Alexander led his men
  Against the Persian king,
He broached a hundred hogsheads, then
  They drank like anything.

166

Drinking Song

They drank by day, they drank by night,
And when they marshalled for the fight
Each put a score of foes to flight—
    Then drank like anything !

    No warrior worth his salt
    But quaffs the mighty malt—
    But quaffs the mighty malt, my boys,
    But quaffs the mighty malt !

When Patrick into Ireland went
    The works of God to do,
It was his excellent intent
    To teach men how to brew.
The holy saint had in his train ·
A man of splendid heart and brain—
A brewer was this worthy swain—
    To teach men how to brew.

    The snakes he drove away
    Were teetotallers they say—
    Teetotallers they say, my boys,
    Teetotallers they say !

A Tankard of Ale

TRIOLET OF DEPLORABLE SENTIMENTS

By Theodore Maynard

I wouldn't sell my noble thirst
For half a dozen bags of gold ;
I'd like to drink until I burst.
I wouldn't sell my noble thirst
For lucre filthy and accurst—
Such treasures *can't* be bought and sold !
I wouldn't sell my noble thirst
For half a dozen bags of gold.

BALLADE OF THE " CHESHIRE CHEESE " IN FLEET STREET [1]

By John Davidson (1837–1909)

I know a home of antique ease
Within the smoky city's pale,
A spot wherein the spirit sees
Old London through a thinner veil.
The modern world so stiff and stale,
You leave behind you when you please,
For long clay pipes and great old ale
And beefsteaks in the " Cheshire Cheese."

[1] From " The Book of the Rhymers' Club."

168

Ballade of the "Cheshire Cheese" in Fleet Street

Beneath this board Burke's, Goldsmith's knees
Were often thrust—so runs the tale—
'Twas here the Doctor took his ease,
And wielded speech that like a flail
Threshed out the golden truth. All hail,
Great Souls! that met on nights like these,
Till morning made the candles pale,
And revellers left the " Cheshire Cheese."

By kindly sense and old decrees
Of England's use they set their sail.
We press to never-furrowed seas,
For vision-worlds we breast the gale;
And still we seek and still we fail,
For still the " glorious phantom " flees.
Ah well! no phantoms are the ale
And beefsteaks of the " Cheshire Cheese."

ENVOI

If doubts or debts thy soul assail,
If Fashion's forms its current freeze,
Try a long pipe, a glass of ale,
And supper at the " Cheshire Cheese."

BALLADE OF LIQUID REFRESHMENT

BY E. C. BENTLEY

LAST night we started with some dry vermouth ;
Some ancient sherry, with a golden glow ;
Then many flagons of the soul of fruit
Such as Burgundian vineyards only grow ;
A bottle each of port was not *de trop ;*
And then old brandy till the east was pink
—But talking makes me hoarse as any crow,
Excuse me while I go and have a drink.

Some talk of Alexander : some impute
Absorbency to Mirabeau-Tonneau ;
Some say that General Grant and King Canute,
Falstaff and Pitt and Edgar Allan Poe,
Prince Charlie, Carteret, Hans Breitmann—so
The list goes on—they say that these could clink
The can, and take their liquor—*A propos !*
Excuse me while I go and have a drink.

Spirit of all that lives, from God to brute,
Spirit of love and life, of sun and snow,
Spirit of leaf and limb, of race and root,
How wonderfully art thou prison'd ! Lo !
I quaff the cup, I feel the magic flow,
And Superman succeeds to Missing Link,
(I say, " I quaff " ; but am I quaffing ? No !
Excuse me while I go and have a drink.)

170

A Ballade of an Anti-Puritan

Hullo there, Prince ! Is that you down below,
Kicking and frying by the brimstone brink ?
Well, well ! It had to come some time, you know.
Excuse me while I go and have a drink.

A BALLADE OF AN ANTI-PURITAN

By G. K. Chesterton

They spoke of Progress spiring round,
Of Light and Mrs. Humphry Ward—
It is not true to say I frowned,
Or ran about the room and roared ;
I might have simply sat and snored—
I rose politely in the club
And said, " I feel a little bored ;
Will someone take me to a pub ? "

The new world's wisest did surround
Me ; and it pains me to record
I did not think their views profound,
Or their conclusions well assured ;
The simple life I can't afford,
Beside, I do not like the grub—
I want a mash and sausage, " scored "—
Will someone take me to a pub ?

171

A Tankard of Ale

I know where Men can still be found,
Anger and clamorous accord,
And virtues growing from the ground,
And fellowship of beer and board,
And song, that is a sturdy cord,
And hope, that is a hardy shrub,
And goodness, that is God's last word—
Will someone take me to a pub ?

ENVOI

Prince, Bayard would have smashed his sword
To see the sort of knights you dub—
Is that the last of them—O Lord—
Will someone take me to a pub ?

A BALLADE OF PROFESSIONAL PRIDE
(Dedicated to Lance-Corporal Fielding of the 5th H.L.I.)

By Cecil Chesterton (1879–1918)

You ask me how I manage to consume
So many beers and whiskies multiplied ;
Why I can stand as rigid as a broom
While others gently sway from side to side ;
Why from the phrase " Ferriferous Vermicide "
My tongue, all unembarrassed, does not shrink ?
—Hear then my city's boast, my calling's pride :
It was in Fleet Street that I learnt to drink.

A Ballade of Professional Pride

Not mine the glory. From the narrow tomb
Call the strong voices of dead men that plied
Their starveling trade along the Street of Doom,
And on its heedless walls were crucified ;
Yet grasped a little laughter ere they died,
Drowned deep in dole and debt and printer's ink,
And with proud note above their torment cried :
" It was in Fleet Street that I learnt to drink ! "

The strong have lived. Alas ! through Eden's bloom
I watch the cocoa-coloured Serpent glide.
The mighty drinkers of old time make room
For prigs in whom the very soul has dried.
Forget them ! For us two the world is wide.
Here's to our comrades ! To the boys that clink
The glass from Asiago to Coxsyde !—
It was in Fleet Street that I learnt to drink.

Envoi

(To a newspaper proprietor)
Prince, you have taken bribes, blackmailed and lied ;
Your horrid vices to the Heavens stink.
Yet by this thing our craft is justified—
It was in Fleet Street that I learnt to drink.

BALLADE IN PRAISE OF ARUNDEL

(Made after a walk through Surrey and Sussex)

BY THEODORE MAYNARD

I've trudged along the Pilgrims' Way,
    And from St. Martha's Hill looked down
O'er Surrey woods and fields which lay
    Green in the sunlight. On the crown
Of Hindhead and the Punchbowl's brink
    Of no good thing I've been bereaven :
But Arundel's the place for drink—
    The pubs keep open till eleven.

White chalk cliffs and the stubborn clay
    Are thrown about, and many a town
Breaks on the sight like breaking day ;
    But after all, who but a clown
Could Arundel with Midhurst link,
    Where men go dry from two till seven ?
In *Arundel* (no truth I'll shrink)
    The pubs keep open till eleven.

A great cool church where men can pray
    Secure from misbelieving frown ;
And in the square, I beg to say,
    The beer is strong and rich and brown.

Nottingham Ale

Some poor misguided people think
   Petworth's the spot that's nearest Heaven :
In *Arundel* the ale pots clink—
   The pubs keep open till eleven.

L'ENVOI

Duke, at the dreadful Judgment Day
   Your soul will surely be well shriven,
For then all angel trumps shall bray,
   He kept pubs open till eleven!

I'VE BIN TO PLYMOUTH [1]

I'VE bin to Plymouth, and I've bin to Doover,
I've bin ramblin, boys, all de wurld oöver,
Over, and over, and over, and oöver,
Drink up your liquor and turn yur cup over.
Over and over, and over, and oöver.
De liquor's drink't up, and de cup is turned oöver.

NOTTINGHAM ALE [2]

WHEN Venus, the goddess of beauty and love,
   Arose from the froth that swam on the sea,
Minerva sprang out of the cranium of Jove,
   A coy, sullen dame, as most authors agree :

[1] From F. E. Sawyer's Lecture on Sussex Songs and Music, 1885.
[2] Chappell's Collection.

175

A Tankard of Ale

But Bacchus, they tell us (that prince of good fellows),
Was Jupiter's son : pray attend to my tale.
For they who thus chatter mistake quite the matter,
He sprang from a barrel of Nottingham ale.
Nottingham ale, boys, Nottingham ale,
No liquor on earth is like Nottingham ale !

Ye Bishops and Curates, Priests, Deacons, and Vicars,
When once you have tasted you'll own it is true,
That Nottingham ale is the best of all liquors,
And none understood what is good like to you.
It dispels ev'ry vapour, saves pen, ink, and paper,
For, when you've a mind in the pulpit to rail,
'Twill open your throats ; you may preach without notes,
When inspir'd with a bumper of Nottingham ale:
Nottingham ale, boys, Nottingham ale, etc.

Ye Doctors, who more execution have done
With powders and potion and bolus and pill,
Than hangman with halter, or soldier with gun,
Or miser with famine, or lawyer with quill ;
To despatch us the quicker, you forbid us malt liquor,
Till our bodies consume and our faces grow pale ;
Let him mind you who pleases—what cures all disease is
·A comforting glass of good Nottingham ale.
Nottingham ale, boys, Nottingham ale,
No liquor on earth is like Nottingham ale !

WARRINGTON ALE [1]

Your doctors may boast of their lotions,
  And ladies may talk of their tea ;
But I envy them none of their potions :
  A glass of good stingo for me.
The doctor may sneer if he pleases,
  But my receipt never will fail ;
For the physic that cures all diseases
  Is a bumper of Warrington ale.

D'ye mind me, I once was a sailor,
  And in different countries I've been ;
If I lie, may I go for a tailor,
  But a thousand fine sights I have seen.
I've been crammed with good things like a wallet,
  And I've guzzled more drink than a whale ;
But the very best stuff to my palate
  Is a glass of your Warrington ale.

When my trade was upon the salt ocean,
  Why, there I got plenty of grog,
And I liked it, because I'd a notion
  It set one's good spirits agog ;
But since upon land I've been steering,
  Experience has altered my tale,
For nothing on earth is so cheering
  As a bumper of Warrington ale.

[1] From Harland's " Ancient Ballads and Songs of Lancashire."

A Tankard of Ale

Into France I have oftentimes followed,
    And once took a trip into Spain ;
And all kinds of liquors I've swallowed,
    From spring water up to champagne.
But the richest of wines to my thinking,
    Compared with good stingo is stale ;
For there's nothing in life that's worth drinking
    Like a bumper of Warrington ale.

WEST SUSSEX DRINKING SONG

By Hilaire Belloc

They sell good beer at Haslemere
    And under Guildford Hill.
At Little Cowfold as I've been told
    A beggar may drink his fill :
There is a good brew in Amberley too,
    And by the bridge also ;
But the swipes they take in at the Washington Inn
    Is the very best Beer I know.

Chorus.

With my here it goes, there it goes,
    All the fun's before us :
The Tipple's aboard and the night is young,
The door's ajar and the Barrel is sprung,
I am singing the best song ever was sung
    And it has a rousing chorus.

Drinking Song

If I were what I never can be,
　The master or the squire :
If you gave me the hundred from here to the sea,
　Which is more than I desire :
Then all my crops should be barley and hops,
　And did my harvest fail
I'd sell every rood of mine acres I would
　For a belly-full of good ale.

Chorus.

With my here it goes, there it goes,
　All the fun's before us :
The Tipple's aboard and the night is young,
The door's ajar and the Barrel is sprung,
I am singing the best song ever was sung
　And it has a rousing chorus.

DRINKING SONG [1]

By Hilaire Belloc

On Sussex hills where I was bred,
When lanes in autumn rains are red.
Where Arun tumbles in his bed,
And busy great gusts go by ;
When branch is bare in Burton Glen
And Bury Hill is a whitening, then

[1] From "The Four Men."

179

A Tankard of Ale

I drink strong ale with gentlemen ;
  Which nobody can deny, deny,
    Deny, deny, deny, deny,
     Which nobody can deny !

In half-November off I go,
To push my face against the snow,
And watch the winds wherever they blow,
  Because my heart is high ;
Till I settle me down in Steyning to sing
Of the women I met in my wandering,
And of all that I mean to do in the spring,
  Which nobody can deny, deny,
    Deny, deny, deny, deny,
     Which nobody can deny !

Though times be rude and weather be rough,
And ways be foul and fortune tough,
We are of the stout South Country stuff,
That never can have good ale enough,
  And do this chorus cry !
From Crowboro' Top to Ditchling Down,
From Hurstpierpoint to Arundel Town,
The girls are plump and the ale is brown :
  Which nobody can deny, deny,
    Deny, deny, deny, deny !
     If he does he tells a lie !

LATIN SONGS

MIHI EST PROPOSITUM [1]

By Walter Mapes (Archdeacon of Oxford)
(circa 1145–1205)

Mihi est propositum in taberna mori
Vinum sit appositum morientis ori,
Ut dicant, cum venerint Angelorum chori,
" Deus sit propitius huic potatori."

Poculis accenditur animi lucerna,
Cor imbutum nectare volat ad superna,
Mihi sapit dulcius vinum in taberna
Quam quod aquâ miscuit praesulis pincerna.

Suum cinque proprium dat natura munus:
Ego nunquam potui scribere jejunus;
Me jejunum vincere posset puer unus,
Sitim et jejunium odi tanquam funus.

Unicinque proprium dat natura donum.
Ego versus faciens vinum bibo bonum,
Et quod habent melius dolia cauponum
Tale vinum generat copiam sermonum.

[1] From Sir Alexander Croke's " Essay on Rhyming
Latin Verse."

A Tankard of Ale

Tales versus facio quale vinum bibo ;
Nihil possum scribere nisi sumpto cibo,
Nihil valet penitus quod jejunus scribo,
Nasonem post calices carmine præibo.

Mihi nunquam spiritus prophitiae datur
Nisi tunc cum fuerit venter bene satur ;
Cum in arce cerebri Bacchus dominatur,
In me Phoebus irruit ac miranda fatur.

DE ADMIRANDIS VIRI VIRTUTIBUS [1]

Quicunque vult esse frater,
Bibat bis, ter, et quater ;
Bibat semel, et secundo,
Donec nihil sit in fundo.
Bibat hera, bibat herus,
Ad bibendum nemo serus :
Bibat iste, bibat illa,
Bibat servus cum ancilla.
Et pro Rege, et pro Papa
Bibe vinum sine aqua.
Et pro Papa et pro Rege :
Bibe vinum sinc lege :
Haec una est lex Bacchica,
Bibentium spes unica.

[1] Twelfth century   From Sir Alexander Croke's "Essay on
Rhyming Latin Verse."

BACK AND SIDE GO BARE, GO BARE! [1]

(Translated by Dr. Maginn)

Non possum multum edere,
  Quia stomachus est nullus;
Sed volo vel monacho bibere,
  Quanquam sit huic cucullus.
Et quamvis nudus ambulo,
  De frigore non est metus;
Quia semper zytho vetulo
  Ventriculus est impletus.
Sint nuda dorsum, latera—pes, manus algens sit,
Dum ventri veteris copia zynthi novive fit.

Assatum nolo, tostum volo,
  Vel pomum igni situm;
Nil pane careo, parvum habeo
  Pro pane appetitum.
Me gelu, nix, vel ventus vi
  Afficerent injuria;
Haec sperno, ni adesset mi
  Zythi veteris penuria.
Sint nuda, etc.

Et uxor Tibie, quae semper sibi
  Vult quaerere zythum bene,
Ebibit haec persaepe, nec
  Sistit, dum madeant genae.

[1] From Marchant's " In Praise of Ale."

A Tankard of Ale

Et mihi tum dat cantharum,
   Sic mores sunt bibosi;
Et dicit " Cor, en ! impleor
   Zythi dulcis et annosi."
Sint nuda, etc.

   Nunc ebibant, donec nictant,
      Ut decet virum bonum;
   Felicitatis habebunt satis,
      Nam zythi hoc est donum.
   Et omnes hi, qui canthari
      Sunt haustibus laetati,
   Atque uxores vel juniores
      Vel senes, Diis sint grati.
Sint nuda dorsum, latera—pes, manus algens sit,
Dum ventri veteris copia zythi novive fit.

INDEX OF FIRST LINES

A Tankard of Ale

Index of First Lines

A Tankard of Ale

PRINTED BY WILLIAM BRENDON AND SON, LTD., PLYMOUTH, ENGLAND

CARVEN FROM
THE
LAUREL TREE

ESSAYS BY

THEODORE MAYNARD

3s. 6d. net.

❡ "Witty, critical, learned, sympathetic—
everything but prosy and dull."—*To-Day*.

❡ "Most companionable."
The Liverpool Post.

❡ "Lively and sparkling."
The Birmingham Post.

OXFORD ✎ B. H. BLACKWELL.

VISION IN NEW POETRY.

THE RED, RED DAWN. By James Mackereth. Foolscap 8vo, boards. 3s. 6d. net.

"Poetry first and last. A model of high thinking and achieved desire."—*Daily Chronicle.*

"At his best, and his best is good indeed."—*Athenæum.*

"A number of poems of very noteworthy quality in their idealism, their purity of feeling and rare virility of phrase. These place him in the little circle of influential poets of our day upon whom there rests a moral and spiritual as well as a literary responsibility."
Yorkshire Post.

AS THE LEAVES FALL. By Capt. J. M. Courtney, R.A.M.C. Crown 8vo, boards. 3s. 6d. net.

"In the forefront of our young poets. . . . There are passages of rare and surpassing beauty all through the book. . . . Since the publication of Mr. Masefield's 'Lollingdon Downs' we have not encountered a more compelling poetic philosophy and a more serious strain of thought than this of Capt. Courtney's. . . . He is a maturer poet than Rupert Brooke, with a clearer insight into the deeps of human nature."—*Aberdeen Journal.*

"New and individual, beaten out of newly-won ore into fresh shapes. . . . An intensely religious note all through the book."—*The Times.*

THEIR DEAD SONS. By J. M. Hay. Crown 8vo, boards. 3s. 6d. net.

"One of the small books of the war that is really great. . . . Mr. Hay has given us something that is nobler than poetry in his pages of unshackled thought," is the *Sheffield Independent's* opinion.

"It expresses fully and eloquently the thoughts and emotions of all for whom the war has brought new sorrows and new visions of the wonder and greatness of humanity," is *The Times's* adequate description of a most timely book, that is now being reprinted to meet a general demand.

WEST WIND DAYS. By May O'Rourke. Boards. 2s. 6d. net. The latest addition to "The Little Books of Georgian Verse."

"The lovely simplicity of Miss O'Rourke, who has learnt the double secret of religion—the meaning of praise and the meaning of pain."—Theodore Maynard in *The New Witness.*

ERSKINE MACDONALD, LTD., LONDON, W.C. 1

Lightning Source UK Ltd.
Milton Keynes UK
UKHW020014100223
416721UK00002B/480